THE HILL OF AFFLUENCE

A THE HILL OF FFLUENCE

To John,

With Best Wishes

Tim Tilden-Smith

T. C. TILDEN-SMITH

AuthorHouse™ UK Ltd.
1663 Liberty Drive
Bloomington, IN 47403 USA
www.authorhouse.co.uk
Phone: 0800.197.4150

© 2013 by T. C. Tilden-Smith. All rights reserved.

No part of this book may be reproduced, stored in a retrieval system, or transmitted by any means without the written permission of the author.

Published by AuthorHouse   08/01/2013

ISBN: 978-1-4918-0064-5 (sc)
ISBN: 978-1-4918-0063-8 (hc)
ISBN: 978-1-4918-0065-2 (e)

Any people depicted in stock imagery provided by Thinkstock are models, and such images are being used for illustrative purposes only.
Certain stock imagery © Thinkstock.

This book is printed on acid-free paper.

Because of the dynamic nature of the Internet, any web addresses or links contained in this book may have changed since publication and may no longer be valid. The views expressed in this work are solely those of the author and do not necessarily reflect the views of the publisher, and the publisher hereby disclaims any responsibility for them.

This reference book is dedicated to my grandchildren,
Amelia and George Smitheram.

My thanks are due to my wife, Mary,
for her constant encouragement, which enabled me to complete the book,

and to

Sue Le Gallez,
for her patience and ability to convert my scribbling into the final typed manuscript.

Contents

Introduction 1
Politics 7
    Constitutional Monarchies 7
    Democratic Republics 12
    The European Union 16
    Communist Regimes and Dictatorships 23
Economics 27
Property Investment 35
Capitalism and The Stock Exchange 41
Starting a Business 49
Deposits and Treasury Stocks 55
Stock Exchange Investment 65
    Collective Investment Vehicles 67
    Passive Investment Vehicles 73
    Investment in the Stock Market 74
Direct Investment 79
    Online Stockbroking 80
Research and Analysis 85
The "Tilden Theory" 91
About the Author 107

Introduction

My first investments were made out of desperation. At the time, I was a cadet in the Shaw Savill and Albion Shipping Company, which operated passenger and cargo ships to Australia and New Zealand. In those days-early post-World War II—cadets' pay was derisory. Admittedly, as our Marine Superintendent never failed to remind us, we had free board and accommodation. Nevertheless, £7 a month, which included £5 a month War Risk money, was not enough to go ashore and entertain members of the fairer sex.

My pay did increase slowly over my three years as a cadet, but it was still very low. I scratched my head and tried to find a way of earning some extra cash. When we were on the New Zealand coast, it was possible to work as a "seagull". This was the name given to non-union members of the Stevedores' Union. It was hard physical work, which I enjoyed, and the pay was excellent. The Chief Officer of the cargo ship I was on at the time was very understanding and let me spend as much of my off duty time as I wanted working as a seagull. It was usually unloading or loading cargo onto my own ship.

By 1949, international trade was booming as people, particularly in England and Europe, were fed up with austerity and wanted to see tropical fruits and exotic oriental goods in the shops again.

This is when I realised I was in a good position to be an international trader. I was on a ship travelling around the world. There was space for me to store some goods, and I had no travelling expenses! I had just passed my Second Mate's exam and joined a new shipping company called P&O. In addition to their Australia route, they also sailed to the Far East. On returning to the UK, their cargo ships did a side trip to Hamburg, Amsterdam, and Rotterdam.

My first cargo ship was on the Far East run, so I started my profitable trading business. The first call was in Port Said, where the bumboat men were selling handgrips made from camel skin, and I bought several of these and other leather goods. Our next interesting ports were Bombay and Colombo. In Bombay, I was fascinated by the clothes that the ladies wore-very colourful, and their saris, handbags, belts, and shoes proved to be one of my winners. I shipped them back to stores in Guernsey and Jersey, where the sales were astonishingly high.

I knew it was only a fad, but for two years, I made a good return on my investment. The buying side always intrigued me. I would arrive at the wholesale emporium and was always invited to sit in a comfortable chair and given ice cold soft drinks. Then there would be a fashion parade, and I would point out the articles I was interested in. The girls were beautiful, too, but not for sale! The goods were shipped direct to the Channel Islands, and I never had any complaints about the quality. I expect the fact that I would be returning to Bombay in a few months ensured that the products were exactly as I had seen and ordered.

In Colombo, I bought carved elephants and sapphire jewellery, which I sold in the UK and Australia. My favourite purchase was in Japan. I found what looked like a miniature camera. It was about two inches by one inch by half an inch. It had a button to press like a real camera, but it flicked open a cover on top, which ignited a flame; in fact, it was a cigarette lighter. I sold hundreds of these at a vast profit.

It was fun but purely a side line to make some extra spending money. Some of my shipmates were curious as to how I could afford taxis and nightclubs in Singapore and Sydney. I simply put my forefinger to my head and said, "Inventiveness". As the saying goes, necessity is the mother of invention.

The Hill of Affluence

In 1956, I sat my Master's exam in London and passed it without a problem. I was offered a position as a Chief Officer of a cargo ship going to India and Malaysia. I had other plans, however, due to the fact that I now had a sick wife and a young son. I had been desperately trying to find a shore job whilst I was studying for my Master's certificate. I must have written to fifty British companies, giving them my CV, but if they bothered to respond, it was to say that I had no degree and no commercial experience. This was the depressing truth. I was twenty-six and had no hope of a career other than to go back to sea.

Then, fortuitously, another student told me that a friend of his had got a job working on cathodic protection of ships with an American company called Wallace and Tiernan. I phoned them up and was asked to attend an interview. The Managing Director was very pleasant but said they currently had no vacancies on their shipping side. They did, however, have a position as a sales and service engineer on their water chlorination side. He told me to go round the factory and let him know if I wanted the job. Despite the fact that I was not mechanically minded, and was terrified of the thought of chlorine gas killing me or one of my customers, I accepted the job. It was going to enable me to be home with my wife and son. After six months in the factory learning how the chlorinating machines worked, I was let loose on the customers. I was able to deal with the smaller installations in public and private swimming pools. One day I was sent to a flour mill and learned that bread was only white because the flour was bleached with chlorine.

Then one morning, the phone rang at eight o'clock, and the factory in Chiswick told me that there was a serious chlorine gas leak at Battersea Power Station. I was to cancel all other appointments and go there immediately. I had never been inside a power station before, and when I arrived, it took me at least ten minutes to find the office of the Chief Engineer. Eventually I did and knocked on the door. A deep voice boomed out "Enter!" The Chief Engineer stood by his desk, put his hands together, and said, "Thank God for Wallace and Tiernan". Little did he know that this member of the company would be of little help to him.

He led me to the chlorination room, which was huge; six of our biggest machines were in there, pumping chlorine gas, visible through the large bell jars on top of the machines. The chlorine was used to prevent the build-up of algae in the cooling water, which was still very hot as it entered the River Thames. There was a terrible smell of chlorine when we entered, forcing us to retreat rapidly. Outside, I told him we would have to shut the plant down to locate and repair the chlorine leak. I asked him how much time we had to do it. He said a maximum of two hours, so I told him I would call the factory in Chiswick and ask them to send another engineer over. The man who arrived was their most experienced engineer, and we solved the problem in about an hour; I was saved by the gong!

That incident convinced me that I should find alternative employment or start up a business of my own. I had a friend who had travelled back from Penang on a P&O ship and was working in the London office of the Far East branch of the company. He hated working in London and was keen to start a business. Eventually, we set up an onsite carpet cleaning service. We handed in our notices to our respective employers and bought an American Columbus-Dixon cleaning machine and got cracking. Our business expanded quite rapidly. We built a carpet cleaning factory, bought and sold a dry cleaning business, bought a carpet wholesale business, and started a contract floor covering business. Then after ten years, I decided to sell out to my partner, leave England, and start a new career as a stockbroker in Guernsey.

Ever since leaving the sea, I had wanted to become a stockbroker, but London was virtually a closed shop, especially to someone of my age with no previous experience in the finance sector.

In 1969, England was in an economic downturn thanks to a Labour government headed by Harold Wilson. Income tax on the upper level of a high earner was 98p in the pound.

My own stockbroker phoned me one day and said that there was an opportunity to join the Guernsey office of a Jersey firm of stockbrokers. My wife's parents had returned from India to live in Guernsey in 1947. Every summer we visited them with our two children for a cheap seaside holiday, so I knew the island, knew many people, and decided to go for an interview. My wife was happy to move, so I accepted the Senior Partner's offer of a partnership in three years' time, subject to my passing the Provincial Brokers Stock Exchange (PBSE) exam. I worked in the back office as well as the front office.

I had taught myself accountancy and was able to interpret company accounts. I understood UK tax, and as a result, I passed the required exam within four months of joining the firm.

I duly became a director of Trevor Matthews and Carey Ltd., which had turned the partnership into a limited corporate member of the London Stock Exchange. Coincidentally with "Big Bang" in the City of London in 1986, I originated a deal whereby a major London broker, Hoare Govett, would take our company over. It was complicated by the fact that three Guernsey companies had shares in our business. Eventually, the deal went through. After that, I resigned from Hoare Govett (Channel Islands) Ltd. and became an investment consultant with various firms until I retired in 2003.

In 1990, I started a new business in Guernsey called Archivist, which, I am pleased to say, thanks to my son-in-law's and my daughter's hard work, is a very successful operation. It specialises in archiving, shredding and scanning documents.

I have also held several non-executive directorships, including Morgan Grenfell (Guernsey) Ltd., Cornhill Insurance (Guernsey) Ltd., and Tyndall Overseas Fund in Jersey. I am now a Fellow of the Chartered Institute for Securities and Investment.

I still follow the stock markets and invest for my own and others' savings. My wife has a house in Florida, where I migrate to in the European winter months, so I have a good feel for what is going on in the American economy; I invest about 25 per cent of my assets in American stocks.

I hope that by giving you a brief history of my varied careers, you will feel that the person writing this little book is sufficiently experienced in business, and qualified in investment, to guide you to a prosperous retirement by means of serious personal pension planning. This does not mean that you cannot have fun when you are young, but temper it with intelligent forward thinking about a comfortable life in retirement.

My own investment philosophy is based on what I call the "Tilden theory." In essence, it aims to beat inflation over the course of seven years. All investment decisions should aim to meet that objective. As the book progresses you will see how important this theory is, and how you can best achieve it.

To begin with I have written chapters on politics and economics. I believe it is essential for all investors to have at least a basic knowledge of these subjects. As far as the chapter on political systems is concerned you will be well aware of your own system, so you can skip that section and read the others! That way you will be able to progress faster to the "Tilden theory" of investment.

Due to the constantly changing political and economic factors which might affect investment plans, you can visit my website www.affluentman.co.uk for regular updates of my views on current affairs and forward investment strategy.

Politics

Comprehension of political systems is essential for businessmen and investors. One could spend a lot of time reading books on politics through the ages. Whilst it may be interesting to learn how different forms of government have evolved, it is the forms that are in place now that are important.

The four main ones to understand are

- constitutional monarchies,
- democratic republics,
- the European Union (EU), and
- communist regimes and dictatorships.

The essential difference between them is that they are headed by a monarch, a president, or a dictator.

Constitutional Monarchies

Great Britain and Northern Ireland are ruled by a monarch. In theory the monarch, as head of state, is all powerful, although in practice the elected members of the House of Commons govern the country. Every five years, or such term as agreed by Parliament, there is an election, and the people vote for their preferred candidate. Normally, one of the major parties collects enough votes to give it a majority. Occasionally, this does not happen, so the various parties see if they can form a coalition with one or more other parties, to give it a working majority.

The members of the winning party, not the public, choose one of the elected members to be prime minister. The prime minister then goes to the monarch and says that he represents his party (or the coalition) and is ready to form a government. The monarch is satisfied, and the new prime minister forms his inner circle, or cabinet. The most important positions in the cabinet are the Chancellor of the Exchequer and the Secretary of State for Foreign and Commonwealth Affairs.

In addition to being head of state, the monarch is head of the Church of England. This still sounds all powerful, but should the monarch refuse to co-operate with the wishes of the government, it would lead to a huge constitutional uproar that could mean the end of the monarchy and its replacement by a republic, as happened in France.

This is extremely unlikely, as the British people in their own way are proud of their monarch and enjoy the panoply, ceremony, prestige, and good will that the apolitical monarch provides.

There will always be some that complain about the cost of maintaining the monarchy and maybe some of the minor royals should not receive any money, but then neither should they then have to devote time to official duties. They should be free to pursue their chosen careers. The monarch's expenses should then not be any more expensive than a president of a republic.

As an example, according to Graham Smith of the *Guardian* newspaper, the total annual bill for the monarch is about £150m. Compare this to a recent visit to India by President Obama of the United States of America. It was reported to have cost $200m, or approximately £130m! The annual cost of the US president is difficult to access, but I feel sure it is more than the cost of the UK monarch.

The main parties in the UK today are the Conservatives, Labour, and Liberal Democrats. The Conservatives are the capitalist party and believe in free enterprise and freedom of choice. The Labourites believe in the state providing for health, education, and other services. The Liberal Democrats tend to lean to the left but surprisingly joined up with the Conservatives in 2010 to form a coalition government.

UK businessmen and investors need to understand these different approaches to government, because they are very relevant when planning investments.

In addition to the House of Commons, there is "the other place", namely the House of Lords. The formation of the two distinct houses goes back to the fourteenth century, when the people's representatives met in the House of Commons and the "Lords Spiritual" (i.e., archbishops, bishops, abbots, and priors), together with the "Lords Temporal" (i.e., the noblemen, consisting of dukes, marquesses, earls, viscounts, and barons), formed the House of Lords.

Over the centuries, there have been many changes to the structure and power of the House of Lords. One of the most significant happened in 1649 when, after the civil war, the monarchy and the House of Lords were abolished. In 1660, after the restoration of Charles II, the House of Lords was reinstated.

In 1999, there were two categories of Peers, namely Hereditary and Lifetime. There was a strong feeling in the country that Hereditary Peers should be abolished. The Labour Government, headed by Tony Blair, introduced the House of Lords Act 1999, which proposed to abolish Hereditary Peers, however some ninety-two existing Hereditary Peers were allowed to remain, pending further reform. There is therefore a majority of Lifetime Peers who are political appointees.

As of now, the reform has not progressed, but the current idea is to have a smaller number of members, 80 per cent of whom are elected and 20 per cent appointed.

The power of the House of Lords has over the years been greatly reduced.

In 1689, the Bill of Rights established Parliament's authority over the monarch. Further acts of Parliament, in 1949 and 1991, limited the length of time delay to debate bills and the power of veto.

Every bill that is passed by both houses then receives royal assent. Queen Elizabeth II said in her Diamond Jubilee speech to the members of both houses that she had signed over 3,000 to date.

The present monarch, Queen Elizabeth II, has so far reigned for sixty years. Queen Victoria reigned for sixty-four years, and Queen Elizabeth I for forty-five years. She has been an outstanding head of state and head of the Commonwealth. Unlike the other two queens who presided over periods of greatness and building of the British Empire, she has seen extraordinary changes in our fortunes. America is now the world's superpower, and Britain has joined the European Union, to the detriment of some of her colonies, especially Australia and New Zealand, who relied on imperial preference for the sale of their agricultural products. She has so far appointed twelve prime ministers and seen twelve presidents hold power in America.

I hope we continue with the present constitutional monarchy, as it acts as a catalyst to unite the population, whereas politicians and presidents are somewhat divisive.

UK elections take place every five years. Sometimes the winning party is the same, but more often there is a change. Because the two main parties' philosophies are so different, it follows that their econometrics are too. Their economic advisers preferably agree with their philosophies but in any case have to adjust their forecasts to strive for equilibrium.

Conservatives' policies are based on the theory that supply and demand will balance each other, even if one side or the other is out of position. Over-regulation is abhorred.

Labour and Liberals' policies tend to move towards government control over everything. Ideologically, they would do away with private education and private health. At times, they have controlled transport and utilities. Without competition, state monopolies' costs get out of control, leading to inflation.

Health and safety regulations are onerous and so are financial regulations. They are both needed but seem to go above their remit, probably because the authorities concerned like expanding their domains. Anyone who has read Parkinson's law will understand the concept.

This involvement in every aspect of our lives means that a Labour government will need to raise money by way of taxation and pay for all the "free" services. That is why they are known as "tax and spend" administrations.

So there is permanent and serious division of philosophies in the UK, which leads to swings in the economy and makes forecasting for investors very difficult. It is business and the middle class who suffer most from "tax and spend" because they are the two easiest and numerically greatest sections of society. There are many ways, some direct and some indirect, by which to raise the additional revenue. Direct taxes are income tax for individuals and corporation tax for businesses. Indirect taxes are VAT, excise duties, and National Health contributions, to name a few.

There are still many constitutional monarchies in Europe; in fact, six of them are members of the European Union.

The monetary policy of the United Kingdom is set by the central bank, namely the Bank of England. It is responsible for trying to control inflation by moving the central base rate up or down. As I write, it is as low as it has ever been at 0.5 per cent. Although it is separate from the government, there has to be a concerted effort to keep inflation under control. It is not practical for the Bank of England to do so by simply adjusting base rates.

Before closing this chapter, I should briefly explain the term "Commonwealth". Prior to World War II, the British Empire was vast. The different countries were ruled and governed by Britain.

After the war, starting with India, many countries pressed for self-rule. Nevertheless, the British, wanting to retain some connections with its former colonies and dominions, formed the Commonwealth of Nations; any country which had been previously part of the British Empire could join. It is presided over by the monarch and is respected worldwide as a forum for fostering good relations, competitive sport, and so on.

Currently, there are fifty-four member countries, the majority of which are republics. There are also many realms. These countries still recognise the monarch as their sovereign.

Democratic Republics

The largest republic is the United States of America. It is also now the most influential country in the world, so it is important to have some knowledge of how it works and has survived for well over two hundred years.

The US Constitution was drafted in 1787 and was ratified by the thirteen original states the following year. It is amazing that such a comparatively short document has survived until this day, with only twenty-seven amendments. In fact, the 18th Amendment, which introduced prohibition of alcohol, was repealed by the 21st Amendment, so there are only twenty-five left. The first ten of these Amendments are known collectively as the Bill of Rights, which was ratified in 1791. Of these, the first two are best known and relate to freedom of speech and the right to bear arms.

The Constitution consists of seven articles:

Article 1. The Legislative Branch
Article 2. The Executive Branch
Article 3. The Judicial Branch

Article 4. The States
Article 5. Amendments
Article 6. Debts, Supremacy, Oaths
Article 7. Ratification

Not counting the amendments, there are only 4,400 words in the original Constitution. On reading it in detail, it is amazing that it is so concise yet so comprehensive.

The most controversial amendment is the second, which states "A well regulated Militia, being necessary to the security of a free State, the right of the people to keep and bear Arms, shall not be infringed". These days this amendment has been abused by criminals and individuals who legally own a variety of firearms, including automatic pistols with magazines holding dozens of rounds. Because military weapons have advanced so much since 1791, it might be construed that individuals need anti-tank guns, flamethrowers, and so on. It is high time this amendment was updated; as the original was made to enable Americans to defend themselves from the British, perhaps a guarantee from Queen Elizabeth II that Britain will never again invade America would help to ease their fears!!

The Legislative Branch is vested in the Congress, which consists of a Senate and a House of Representatives. The Senate is composed of two senators from each state. The House of Representatives is composed of members elected every two years. The number of members varies from state to state, being based on the size of their population.

The Executive Branch is, simply, the president. He has limited powers but is commander in chief of the military and as such can commit America to a war. He appoints a vice president and forms an administration, the two most important members of which are the secretary of state and the secretary to the treasury. He can also appoint judges to the Supreme Court.

The Judicial Branch is headed by the Supreme Court; appointees may hold their position for life.

The object of having separation of power between these three branches is known as "checks and balances." It is basically a system that means at least two of the three have to agree to any proposals. It is slightly inefficient because it slows down action, but it does ensure that no one branch has too much power.

Beneath this federal level, each state also has the same branches.

The president is elected by the public vote and by the Electoral College. The latter was in place because initially the public were not considered to be bright enough to arrive at the best answer. So the Electoral College was set up. It consists of electors, generally being elected by the individual states' political party committees. The number of such electors is equal to the number of representatives the state has in the House of Representatives, plus one for each of its senators.

At the moment, there are 538 electors, so 270 votes are needed to give one presidential candidate a majority. This system, however, can and does throw up anomalies. For instance, in 1876, an ancestor of mine, namely Samuel J. Tilden, was the Democratic candidate. He won the popular vote by 4,300,590 to his opponent Rutherford Hayes, who received 4,036,298 votes. However, there was an overturn of this when the Electoral College voted by 185 to 184 to defeat Tilden, and Hayes was elected. The same thing happened in 2000 when Al Gore won the popular vote but the Electoral College won it for George W. Bush by 271 to 266.

One day the Electoral College may be abolished, but there are a lot of pros and cons to consider.

The president is elected for a four-year term and can then stand once more for a further four years only. Representatives are elected every two years, and one-third of senators are elected every two years, which means in effect that they can be in office for six years before standing for re-election.

Both representatives and senators can be re-elected as many times as the electors vote for them. Supreme Court judges are appointed for life by the president, with the approval of the Senate. But first the Senate Judiciary Committee interviews the nominee and then approves the appointment by a simple majority. Their recommendation goes then to a vote on the floor of the Senate and finally to the president.

Each state follows the same rules.

There are effectively only two parties in America, namely Republicans and Democrats. There are a few Independents but not enough to prevent an outright win for a major party. Another important point to remember is that both Democrats and Republicans are essentially capitalist. This means they are pro business and free enterprise. The Republicans are generally for less regulation and less government, whilst the Democrats are known as the "tax and spend" party because they want more control of social services, health, and education.

America has a central bank, known as the Federal Reserve Bank. It operates as a lender of last resort, and its chairman and the Federal Open Market Committee are responsible for setting interest rates. In times of economic downturn, "the Fed" can effectively print money to oil the wheels of industry. The term now used for this operation is "Quantitative Easing". The chairman also has to brief Congress on the economy from time to time.

Their debt is currently the highest it has ever been, and one of the bodies that monitors such things as a country's indebtedness has recently downgraded US government debt. Since they have also downgraded so many others, especially several European countries, it has really not affected the Treasury market, and the US dollar is still regarded as the world's safest currency.

The European Union

This is a new type of government, which is effectively a government of governments, led by a president. It is a most complicated union and one which would have been much better if, from the word "go", the founders had said they would create a United States of Europe based on a constitution similar to America's. It did not happen because, for a start, several potential members were constitutional monarchies like the UK. Apart from that insoluble problem, other states did not want to give up their sovereignty or right to determine their own rules in any aspect of government. So what happened?

The history goes back to early post-war years. Europe was struggling to recover from a terrible conflict which had destroyed virtually everything. In 1949, the Council of Europe was set up by ten countries at the Treaty of London. This must not be confused the Council of the European Union or the European Council, which are EU institutions.

These were the council's aims, as set out in the statute:

Article 1(a)
"The aim of the Council of Europe is to achieve a greater unity between its members for the purpose of safeguarding and realising the ideals and principles which are their common heritage and facilitating their economic and social progress".

Article 1(b)
"This aim shall be pursued through the organs of the Council by discussion of questions of common concern and by agreements and common action in economic, social, cultural, scientific, legal, and administrative matters and in the further realisation of human rights and fundamental freedoms".

The organs of the Council of Europe are:

- The Committee of Ministers
- The Consultative Assembly

Both are served by the Secretariat of the Council of Europe; its base is in Strasbourg.

The Committee of Ministers is comprised of the foreign ministers of member countries, and the Consultative Assembly is comprised of an elected member of the parliament of each member country.

The best known convention created by the Assembly was the European Convention for Human Rights and Fundamental Freedoms. This was adopted by the Council of Europe in 1950, and cases are heard in the European Court of Human Rights based in Strasbourg.

It now has forty-seven member countries. In 1950, the French proposed closer co-operation, and a year later the "Schuman Plan", named after the French Foreign Minister, was set up by six countries. In July 1952, they integrated their coal and steel industries under the title of the European Coal and Steel Community. This arrangement seemed to work well, so in 1957 they decided to expand their co-operation with each other's economic activities and signed the treaty in Rome establishing the European Economic Community (EEC). This treaty formed the basis of the European Union as we know it today.

In 1960, another organisation was founded to provide a framework for the liberalisation of trade in goods between member states. The UK was one of the members. It was named the European Free Trade Association (EFTA). This was to act as an economic counterbalance to the more politically driven EEC. Since then, most members have left to join the EEC. The reason why it took so long for the UK to join the EEC was due to the fact that the French leader, Charles de Gaulle, vetoed British accession. It was only after his death in 1969 that negotiations resumed to enable the UK to join. It finally made it in 1973. Today EFTA consists of Iceland, Liechtenstein, Norway, and Switzerland.

The Treaty of Rome in 1957 set out, amongst other things, the terms of a customs union, which was why the EEC was commonly called "the Common Market". In fact, the Common Market related exclusively to the free movement of goods. The free movement of people, capital, and services was limited. In 1987, the Single European Act was signed; it endeavoured to establish a genuine unified market. The other major agreement in the Treaty of Rome saw the inclusion of the Common Agricultural Policy. This has created almost as many problems as it has solved.

Between 1957 and the next treaty, known as the Treaty of the European Union, popularly known as the Maastricht Treaty, in 1992, a lot of work was done to further integration and to establish layers of governance.

The Council of the European Union is the main decision making body. It represents the member states and is attended by one minister from each state relative to the subjects on the agenda. This is not to be confused with the European Council, whose members are the prime minister or presidents of member states. Their meetings are very important, as they set overall EU policy and settle issues that were not settled at a lower level.

Following on from the Lisbon Treaty, which came into force on 1 December 2009, a president is elected for two and a half years, with an option to continue for a further two and a half years. The first long-term president was a Belgian politician named Herman Van Rompuy. The idea behind this move is that it replaces the previous revolving six-month presidential term, which made it difficult for foreign countries' heads of state to know who they were going to be dealing with.

Then there is the European Commission. This entity has four main roles:

1. To propose legislation to Parliament and the council
2. To manage and implement EU policies and the budget
3. To enforce European law jointly with the Court of Justice
4. To represent the EU on the international stage

Member states each appoint one commissioner. The commissioners may have been government ministers but are honour bound to act in the interests of the union as a whole and not to take instructions from their respective governments. The commission is politically accountable to the president. Its day-to-day operations are looked after by some 20,000 civil servants.

The European Parliament is responsible for passing European laws and for exercising democratic supervision of the other EU institutions, particularly the commission. It also shares with the Council of the European Union the approval of the EU budget.

Members of the European Parliament are elected every five years by their respective citizens. Currently, there are 736 members from twenty-seven EU countries. The number of seats for each country is roughly the same as their populations as a percentage of the whole. For example, Germany has ninety-nine, UK and France seventy-two, and so on.

There is no doubt that it is a cumbersome and extremely expensive type of government.

In 1979, it was considered necessary to align member countries' currencies in some way to deal with their internal accounting. The system was called the European Monetary System (EMS), and the unit of account was the European Currency Unit (ECU).

The system was a limited but flexible one that defined bands between which the bilateral exchange rates could fluctuate. If the member countries' currency fluctuated by more than these bands against the ECU, the members' central banks had to support the rates through open market operations.

This system was the precursor to full currency conversion into the Euro, which took place on 1 January 2002. In preparation for this, the European Central Bank (ECB) was established in 1998. Its primary function was to ensure the smooth running of the economic and monetary union through the European system of the central banks of all members of the EU. However, there is another system called the "Eurosystem", which the ECB and Eurozone member central banks belong to. There is therefore a complication which adds to the confusion. There are two classes of EU members: those that are in the Eurozone and those that still retain their own currencies, like the United Kingdom.

The EU, which now consists of twenty-seven countries, only has seventeen participants in this currency union. With domestic agendas so different to each other, it has been argued that it is virtually impossible for it to survive in its current form.

Following on from the American property market and banking collapse in 2008, the problem migrated to Europe. Ireland was the first member to suffer from an overheated property market and huge problems with its banks, which had enormous debts.

Others followed suit, with Portugal and Spain suffering from the same malaise. However, the problem was really serious when Greek borrowings from outside banks were used to disguise the fact that the country was essentially bankrupt prior to it joining the Eurozone.

The financial structure of the EU is very complicated and ever changing. There are several international financial institutions which essentially fund European industry. The best known are the European Investment Bank and the European Bank for Reconstruction and Development. They raise funds on the international bond market.

The European commission, through the Directorate-General for Economic and Financial Affairs (DG-ECFIN), works on financial integration and assesses whether a member of the EU which wants to join the Eurozone is able to comply with the convergence rules.

There is a much more complicated problem when, instead of financing industry, there is a need to finance weaker nations within the Eurozone.

The European Central Bank is not a lender of last resort, like the US Federal Reserve Bank or the Bank of England. It cannot lend to governments. It is part of the European System of Central Banks, whose main aim is to implement the monetary policy within the whole of the EU.

To endeavour to guarantee the stability of the Euro area, and to give financial assistance to member states in financial difficulties or under serious market pressure, two temporary entities were introduced in May 2010. These were the European Financial Stability Facility (EFSF) and the European Financial Stability Mechanism (EFSM).

On 11 July 2011, the finance ministers of the seventeen Euro area countries signed yet another treaty establishing the European Stability Mechanism (ESM). Once this is ratified, it is expected to take over the operations of the EFSF and the EFSM.

These entities can lend money to governments for them to use to recapitalise their banks, but such loans will have strict conditions attached to them, such as reducing government debt over the period of the loan. It also has to be rubber-stamped by the commission and the ECB. Any funds lent to member countries are partially guaranteed by other member countries, with the exception of member countries already in debt. Germany, being the largest, has to guarantee the highest percentage, which is one of the reasons why it is difficult to find a way of bailing out Spain and Italy. It would have serious repercussions for Germany. Strangely enough, it might end up with Germany leaving the Euro, as it is now by far and away the strongest country in the Eurozone, and many Germans object to depriving themselves to support profligate countries like Greece.

In the case of Greece, there was a special Greek loan facility negotiated. This was different from the loans made to Ireland and Portugal. The facility was provided by a combination of contributions from the Eurozone and the International Monetary Fund (IMF), which also provided some funds for Ireland and Portugal.

The IMF was started in 1944, and its mandate was to ensure the stability of the international monetary system. It also was to encourage economic growth, which in turn would increase living standards and reduce poverty around the world. In my view, it has now shifted its mandate to finance the debts of Eurozone countries on the excuse that it is necessary for global stability. This will inevitably mean that there will be less capital available for poverty-stricken third world countries.

It is funded by its member countries when funds are needed by contributions, roughly according to each country's economic size. The United States of America is the biggest contributor, so it is in effect contributing to the cost of supporting the weaker members of the Eurozone.

The Eurozone has serious financing problems. Spain is the latest country to find itself in a desperate financial state. Their banks are short of capital due to having so much tied up in property. No one really knows whether they have written off all their bad debts. If they had, they would probably be insolvent. Similarly to the United States and Ireland, Spain has an unsustainable property boom, which will take several more years to unwind. Unemployment is the highest in the Western world at 25 per cent. The economy is bad, no one wants to buy Spanish debt, and the government has to pay unsustainable rates of interest on its loans.

The big debate of today is how to prevent a total collapse of the Eurozone. The president of the ECB has sworn that they will do everything in their power to maintain the Euro. Unfortunately, no solid measures have been proposed, so the world awaits further news.

As you will by now realise, it is such an extraordinarily complex financial system, with so many interlocking entities, that to arrive

The Hill of Affluence

at a united agreement on how to protect the Euro currency is more than challenging-it is more like impossible. For instance, the German chancellor and the previous right wing French president presented a strong alliance within the Eurozone, but with a shift to the left in French politics, the strength of the alliance has weakened.

I must leave the European Union at this point, but the reason I have spent more time on it, rather than on other political systems, is that I believe that the success or failure of the Eurozone will have important global repercussions.

Communist Regimes and Dictatorships

The other types of government are those found in Communist countries like Russia and China. It might well be considered foolish to invest in countries with these types of governments, as interest payment on their debts and even the debts themselves could be cancelled without notice. Also foreigners' assets could be sequestered.

The Chinese economy is now one of the biggest in the world, after America. It has recently overtaken Japan.

There is ample opportunity for investment in China, so it is important to understand the basic principles of their form of government.

This Communist regime is known as the People's Republic of China. In fact it is an oligarchy.

At the head of the regime is the Communist Party, which has ruled China since 1949. There are over 60m members of the Communist Party of China, and the governance works its way from the top committee members down through the Politburo, the National People's Congress, to the courts and prosecutors. The Politburo receives input from the Discipline Commission and the party elders. It then disseminates information and advice to the Military Affairs Commission and to the State Council, who in turn deal with the armed forces and the provinces and townships.

It is a very complex system, and it is particularly interesting at this moment in time, when a certain amount of private enterprises are allowed to run alongside the strict Communist ideology. It remains to be seen how this relationship will play out. In fact, China is rapidly becoming the largest industrial nation on earth. In order to protect their raw material supplies, they are investing heavily in many companies in Africa. They are in this respect following along the lines of the European colonialists. They do not, however, become involved in the countries' politics, so the colonialism is purely commercial.

For anyone interested in learning more details of China's political system, I strongly recommend visiting the website www.china.org.cn. On reading part 2, which states the four basic demands for the building of the party, I noticed that the fourth basic principle is to uphold democratic centralism. I feel this is a serious oxymoron.

To my mind, it is the most interesting economy in the world today and presents investors with excellent prospects, albeit with some caution because it still is very much a Communist regime.

Russia is now a republic, not quite Communist and not quite a democratic republic.

Cuba is a Communist country but is run by a dictator.

Venezuela is a straightforward dictatorship.

Then there are some countries where the military took power, such as Chile, and the commander in chief, as instanced by the now deceased General Pinochet, acted as a dictator.

Before investing in any country with a Communist regime or a dictator, you will need to examine their record with respect to inward investment. There are many varieties of political regimes; in some, like South Africa, politicians have been democratically elected, although the investments might be good, such as gold mines, you have to consider potential labour problems and adverse currency movements. Now I am blending investment with politics, so it is time to move on to another subject.

Economics

Not a single day passes without a mention in the media of the economy or economics. There are thousands of economists around the world, with expensive and extensive educations in all aspects of finance behind them. What do economists talk about? Well, the economy, stupid! Ask them to define the word "economy", and they will give you such a convoluted answer that you will be even more confused than you were before you asked the question.

Is economics really as complex a subject as they make it out to be? Well, yes and no. I propose breaking it down into four categories. The principle is the same, but as we progress through the categories, we will see how the variables make economic forecasting as imprecise as weather forecasting.

In a sense, we are all economists, because we all have to manage our finances in such a manner that we do not become bankrupt. In other words we, as "domestic economists", have to "live within our means". This phrase, which embodies the entire problem associated with economics, needs to be adhered to. As children, we learn that our pocket money has to be allocated to our most urgent needs, whether it be to save until we have enough to buy a special object or just to blow on sweets. Once our education is finished, we find a job and eventually move out of our family home. This is when we really start being fully fledged domestic economists.

We are lucky in that our income is fixed. By this, I mean we earn a salary if we are employed in a full-time position. Our net earnings after tax and Social Security deductions are paid into our bank accounts. It is this net (after deductions) amount that's ours to live off. This is when we need to budget. Budgeting to most young people is an anathema and something for their parents or their employers to worry about. I assure you that the earlier in life you understand the need to have a weekly, monthly, or annual budget, the more straightforward your life will be.

Domestic economists' budgeting is made very simple when their income is fixed. It can become more complicated if part of their income is salary and part bonus. Assuming in the first instance that it is fixed, then you need to list all your known expenses which have to be paid. These are fixed expenses and include such items as rent, travelling expenses, and insurance premiums. Other expenses such as food are variable expenses. Usually, to begin with, whatever is left over is spent on self-enjoyment, and why not, because we are only young once! However, as time goes on, our liabilities increase and we have to ensure that they do not exceed our income. Our first major purchase will probably be a car, and this will normally mean taking out a loan, as we will not have saved enough to purchase it for cash. It is important to realise at this critical stage in our life that a loan is not a gift. Not only do we have to repay the principal, but there will be interest as well. Does our net income after all taxes and essential expenditure leave us with enough credit to cover the purchase cost, plus interest? If the answer is yes, then we are "living within our means".

This is so basic and so easily understood that domestic economists are more fortunate than other categories. As they age, they will probably have children. They then face their biggest economic decision. Should they rent or buy their accommodation? The argument for owning is compulsive. Rent that you pay to your landlord goes towards paying off the loan he has with his bank. It therefore must be madness not to buy and use the rent money we would have paid to the landlord, to pay off our own mortgage. This is absolutely true, and once again the only financial aspect that you

The Hill of Affluence

need to worry about is whether your surplus income after essential expenditure leaves more than sufficient to service the loan repayments and interest on the mortgage.

One more important point for the domestic economist: from the day you receive your first pay cheque, you should set aside some money and put it into your savings account. This "rainy day" account is not only an easy way of saving, it also gives you a sense of security, knowing that it can cover some vital but unexpected expenses such as a medical bill.

Now we move up the ladder to the point where there are variables on both income and expenditure. This relates to small businesses and partnerships. The directors are also the principal shareholders of these small businesses. I call such people "business economists". They should be governed by the same principle of living within one's means. All businesses have to try to do this, but the variables make it more difficult so they have to set serious budgets for the business. It is vitally important to accurately assess the potential income from sales and services so that the planned expenditure does not exceed this amount. Sales professionals are eternal optimists, so their forecasts should be trimmed a little. If they reach their targets, all well and good, but if they do not and your expenditure has exceeded the sales, you will have a problem.

Businesses need capital, and what some entrepreneurs do not understand is that as their business grows, they inevitably need more capital. The usual way is to start with your own capital and then approach your bankers. They will want a business plan for the future, a personal guarantee, even a transfer of some of the business assets into their name. Increased turnover is good, but it has ruined many new businesses. It is known as "over trading", and if the business owners have not arranged finance to cover the gap between obtaining payments from customers and payments to suppliers, they will soon find the bank account is overdrawn. It is such a basic fact, yet so many new and growing businesses face this situation.

At all times, forward planning and budgeting are vital for any business but especially in the first few years until profits start flowing in.

During my life, I have been amazed at the way successful entrepreneurs have made their fortunes from so many different activities. A lot of post-WWII entrepreneurs made their fortunes from property. One I particularly admire is Sir Donald Gosling, who started buying or renting bomb sites in London after the war and charging people to park their cars. He ended up owning National Car Parks and also owns, to my nautical eye, one of the most attractive yachts in the world, called *Leander G*.

What I am saying is that there are always opportunities to start a business. You need to have determination, self-confidence, and a bright idea that few other people have thought of. It is you who has to drive the business. You can hire salespeople and accountants. In a way, I see a successful entrepreneur as being similar to the conductor of a symphony orchestra. Both bring their performances to perfection.

Now, unfortunately, economics becomes seriously more complicated as we look at my next category, which is the "corporate economist". This group is one step up the business ladder, in that they are directors running big businesses with outside shareholders. Once again, the mantra is the same: live within one's means. This is much more difficult to plan for, as the variables will have increased dramatically. There are two types of large public company: the ones that trade domestically and others that trade internationally.

The domestic ones, especially service companies, have plenty of variables to contend with, but they do not have currency conversions to worry about. Their budgets are therefore comparatively easy to prepare. The directors are responsible to the shareholders to provide steady growth in capital value and rising income. If they fail, they can, and do, lose their jobs. They have to be prepared to sack staff in an economic downturn, to reduce stocks, to slow down opening of new stores, to spend less on research and development, and so on. Equally, when the economic climate improves, they need to reverse these measures. Not all will do this, so the profits plunge and share prices drop until such time as the downturn measures take effect and show up as greater profitability on reduced turnover.

Companies can make money by organic growth, by acquisitions, or by a combination of the two.

Whatever the directors of these companies do, they must live within their means. Unlike the directors/owners whose decisions directly affect their own pockets, the directors of a public company are using banks' and shareholders' money to build their empires and their potential rewards by way of bonuses. Whilst the majority of directors put their shareholders first, there are some who enter into very risky ventures or acquisitions. Sometimes I believe deals are not recommended by directors because the terms they have tried to negotiate for themselves have failed. These failed bids usually end up being detrimental to shareholders' wealth.

The international trading companies such as oil, pharmaceutical, and industrial manufacturers have many variables to contend with, the most difficult being variation in currencies and fluctuation in commodity prices. Finance directors of these companies have to be quick on their feet to do forward deals which help to even out fluctuations and produce a rising trend in profits. This is not always possible, which is one of the reasons why share prices of these companies are so volatile. These directors also rely on economists who specialise in various fields and try to predict future movements in prices of raw materials, currency movements, and consumer confidence. There are so many economic forecasts that it is exceptionally difficult for them all to be right. The hope is that they are right more often than they are wrong.

Now we arrive at our last group, which I call "political and global economists". Politicians come in many different hues: blue for conservative, red for socialist, yellow for liberal, and green for environmentalists. Because their agendas are so different, their economic models are too theoretical. At the end of the day, they too have to have policies that enable them to allow their country to live within its means.

However, they have a huge advantage over individuals and corporations in that they can ask their central bank to print money. This is often done in times of economic stress. Unfortunately, in the end, nothing in life is free, and debts have to be repaid, even by governments. This leads to severe reductions in government expenditure, combined with increases in taxation. It can be very painful and protracted.

Politics and economics are like oil and water; the two just do not mix. Politicians have economists advising them not only on domestic economic issues but also on global issues that are likely to affect their own economy. The problem for politicians is that they try to balance good economic sense with their desire to be re-elected. Sadly, the economic policies are usually steered towards the latter.

This is where economics becomes so complicated and technical that not even economists can agree on many issues. I think of domestic, business, and corporate economists as "practical economists", whereas I tend to think of political and global economists as "theoretical economists". I think like this because once politics are involved, there are so many variables that the theories propounded cannot be relied on to solve national issues, let alone the world's economic problems. Most economists' energy is expended during economic downturns. After all, when things are booming, we do not need to live within our means. Our tax revenues are high, government spending is high, everyone is high, and economists take a back seat.

This had unfortunate results in the UK, due to Gordon Brown's determination to stop booms and busts-he was chancellor in boom times and prime minister in the biggest bust since World War II.

What I am saying is that excesses turn into downturns. Economists advising governments have a lot to answer for. Now they are propounding many economic theories to lift the world out of recession; the best known theory in recent times being the Keynesian theory. This essentially states that in a recession, if the private sector spending dries up, the public sector has to spend more in order for the economy to recover.

To try and understand why we constantly have booms and busts, it is vital to understand the business angle. We start in a period of equilibrium, which means that supply equals demand. There is near full employment and home incomes are stable, so individuals have a feel-good attitude and spend money on goods and services. This spending is good, but if it is overdone, there is pressure on the suppliers to match demand, so prices go up, and because there is a shortage of labour in the service providers, their prices go up too. It does not take long for the cycle to move to the point where demand falls off. Manufacturers and retailers see an increase in stock levels, and the service sector suffers as money becomes tighter.

One of the major causes of recession has been speculative building of property. Banks have notoriously cashed in on housing bubbles by lending to all and sundry without due regard to the ability of borrowers to maintain their mortgage repayments, overlooking the fact that historically all booms in the property market have ended in disaster.

When the downturn comes in the property sector, it leads to demand for white goods and furnishings to fall off. People start getting worried about the future as house prices fall. The feel-good factor is replaced by doom and gloom. Jobs are being lost, and spending turns into saving. This is when the government is likely to move towards replacing the drop in spending by the private sector by increasing expenditure on infrastructure projects. This will create jobs, jobs mean income, income can be spent, and so the cycle gradually returns to a near equilibrium again.

Supply side and trickle-down economics aim to achieve the same result but by reducing taxation on individuals and businesses. The hope is that the additional retained income will be spent by individuals on goods and services and by businesses on expansion in terms of output, which will mean more employees. These are simple measures to take, and normally they will work, but in the modern world, global events distort the picture.

As an example of the problem, just look at the European Union and the Euro currency. Every country using the Euro has different levels of taxation and different views on social security. This had led to huge problems, causing some countries to be supported by the wealthier member states. It is such an obvious fault of the European economic system, yet they make no move towards united policies on these vital economic issues.

Unless they really make an effort soon to rectify these problems, the Euro as we know it is doomed, and with it possibly the European Union itself. Governments can easily upset the global equilibrium by introducing tariffs and quotas for certain imports, by manipulating their currency, and so on. That is why we are now plagued with hordes of economists all propounding solutions for the good of their own positions, without regard to the global consequences.

Can we expect that one day the world will work as a balanced whole? I fear not, because the equilibrium between supply and demand is too complicated in a super macroeconomic situation.

We are lucky as domestic economists not to have to contend with as many variables. All we have to concentrate our minds on is to live within our means and be sure to save some money for our retirement, by prudent investment planning. The "Tilden theory" of investment guides individual savers towards a happy and prosperous retirement.

Another reason is the totally opposite views of the United States of America and Europe as to how to climb out of the current recession. The United States, guided by the Fed, is adopting the Keynesian theory, which is to spend their way out (never mind the increase in long-term debt), whereas Europe is focusing on reducing government debt by means of strict austerity measures.

Both economic theories cannot be right, and only time will prove which was better.

Property Investment

A real investment is when physical assets are purchased, such as a property. I touched on the subject in the previous chapter. Some countries like Germany seem to encourage people to rent rather than buy their own homes, whereas in other Western countries, individuals strive to own their residences. There are pros and cons which need exploring. In the UK and the USA, many young people leave home to go to university; most, however, start a job. There is a desire to move out of the family home for reasons of privacy. At this young age, there is no chance of buying a flat, apartment, or house, so renting is the only solution. In fact, renting is the sensible solution until one's lifestyle and career are more settled. Many changes of location, based on where one's workplace is, often happen in the early stages of one's career. At some point, a degree of stability will emerge, and amazingly, to their family and friends, there is talk of settling down, even possibly getting married.

This is definitely the time to consider the benefits of buying rather than renting one's accommodation. Either you or your intended spouse or both of you have saved up enough money to place a 10 per cent deposit down with a mortgage company or bank. This is all well and good, but it will leave you with very little savings for a rainy day.

The best time to consider buying is when interest rates are low. With base rates at 0.5 per cent they are unlikely to fall, so right now is a great time. If you do not have enough savings to put down 10 per cent of the cost of the property, you are simply not able to buy. I do have a suggestion, however, which will enable you to proceed without too much difficulty. I suggest you approach your parents and ask them if they would consider lending you the amount of the deposit. You might be surprised to find that they are happy to do so, especially if you are still living at home with them.

Seriously, though, with interest rates so low, it is a wonderful way to help one's children get onto the property ladder. You will also be able to pay them a rate of interest which is better than they can obtain from a deposit and less than you would have to pay from any other lender.

Now comes the exciting time. You have to decide on what type of accommodation you want. It might range from a small flat or apartment near your place of work to a house in the suburbs. Whatever you find, you must be prepared to negotiate. There are plenty of similar properties around, but some are owned by half-hearted sellers and some by desperate sellers. You should do your homework and check with several estate agents in order to assess the right price.

Now that you have narrowed down what you want and determined what the right price is, you need to shop around for the best mortgage deal. There are of course several websites that will help you to narrow down your options.

So, you have your parents and your mortgage company lined up and you know your right price. The next step is to see whether you can afford the repayments plus interest. Obviously, if you are married, your joint incomes should pay the mortgage off by monthly payments. You should not forget, however, that you will now have other expenses that were rolled up into the rent that you were paying. These can be quite a lot and include property tax in America, rates in England, also house and contents insurance. These are fixed expenses. There will also be many variables such as food, clothes, and heating.

In addition to the annual expenses, you will have a considerable outlay to furnish the place properly.

Before visiting your realtor in America or your estate agent in the UK, make sure that you can comfortably afford to furnish the property and afford the fixed and variable annual expenses.

It is always better to buy one or two more bedrooms than you need, especially if you are planning to marry and have children. The reason is that moving involves expense of selling and buying, which is nice for the estate agents and lawyers but not for you. The extra monthly payments will probably be less than the moving expenses.

All that remains now is that you keep fit and keep your job. The former can be covered by insurance, but the latter is a problem that is unforeseen. If it does happen, you will need to let your mortgage company or bank know immediately and hope that they will help you out.

It is only when you look at this aspect of property ownership that you realise how much more advantageous it is to own your own. In addition to acquiring an asset instead of paying good money to a landlord who will use it to pay off his mortgage, you will also have created a painless way of saving.

Some people are so keen on property that they invest in it. There are two main ways to do this. One is to buy and rent out, and the other is to buy and "flip". Flipping, or selling quickly, was very prevalent in the early years of the century when the property market was so overheated that prices were rising almost overnight. This situation does not often occur, so buying for longer term capital appreciation is the normal reason for investing in property.

Most properties bought for this reason are rented out to provide sufficient income to cover all outgoings. Ideally more than this, to give a return on the capital investment equal to current deposit interest rates or a ten year Treasury stock. The reason for using this yardstick is that the property should have increased considerably in ten years, but if it had not, you would still be no worse off than if you had bought a ten-year Treasury stock.

Investment properties do not always achieve a steady income or a capital profit. The tenant can fall on hard times and plead poverty. You are then faced with being ruthless and giving him notice to quit or being humane and giving him a chance to recover. I personally would not like to be in the position of the ruthless landlord, especially if the tenant was married and had a young family. I would only rent to single professional people. In practice, I have never rented out a property and am never likely to. Nevertheless, in good times it can be a very good investment. In bad times, such as we have seen in the property crash of 2006-2007, home buyers as well as property speculators have been left with negative equity. This means that the value of the property has fallen in value by a substantial amount. As an example, let us assume that you purchased a property for £300,000, which is now only worth £200,000. The speculators can hold on for a turnaround or sell and take a loss, depending to some extent on their tax position. I have deliberately avoided writing about tax because it is different from country to country, person to person, and individual to a corporation. Before embarking on a property investment, you should ask a tax accountant whether it is better to invest as an individual or as a corporation or a trust.

What has happened to many home owners is that they are effectively paying £300,000 for something that is only worth £200,000. In many cases, they have ceased paying their monthly payments, so the mortgage company or bank forecloses on the property, which they then own. As a result in America, Ireland, and Spain, the banks are left holding properties they cannot or will not sell. The threat of further foreclosures has also had a negative effect on the property market. Banks are loath to lend unless a substantial part of the purchase price is paid up front. There appears to be no end to the impasse, and property prices are unlikely to rise much in the near future. Because of the surplus of properties held by the banks, there is very limited activity in the building trade.

The solution will be several years down the road when new young buyers come into the market.

We have seen property booms and busts before, and they are always caused by banks lending to people they know have a limited chance of paying off their loans. Also, the speculators were borrowing money and buying up more new homes, especially in Florida and Nevada in the USA and Ireland and Spain in the EU, than they could ever expect to find genuine buyers to pass them on to. The recent crash has been the worst ever and consequently will take longer to unravel.

Commercial property can be a good investment, but in a severe recession, even this is risky.

Current market conditions are in favour of the buyer because interest rates are so low, and I am sure it is a good time to invest for the long term. Rather than investing in one property, it is worth considering investing in shares of a quoted property company or real estate investment trust.

Capitalism and The Stock Exchange

Before investigating the various opportunities open to investors, it is essential to understand the meaning of capitalism.

We live in a capitalist society, where it is considered normal for individuals to have freedom to achieve their dreams. They can choose to work harder and for longer hours in return for higher rewards. Many years ago, there was little control on the rewards, but now taxation controls them to some extent.

For capitalist activities to succeed, there has to be a successful blend of capital and labour. One without the other is not going to work. There is a constant battle, between the entrepreneurs and providers of capital on the one hand, and the workers they employ represented by trade unions on the other, as to how the profits of their endeavours should be divided up. The shareholders who have provided the ideas and the capital are the spark that starts the enterprise, and the workers are the fuel that keeps the enterprise moving. It is for these reasons that the distribution of profits is a constant source of friction. The capitalists should receive a substantial amount to compensate them for the risk involved. Equally, the workers should receive a living wage, geared to productivity. This is a very loose term, however, and depends on what society considers it to be. Of course, not all the profits are distributed, because to expand the business requires more capital. It is never going to be easy to achieve a fair balance between the participants, and there will be ongoing negotiations to achieve the fairest balance.

Although it has its flaws, capitalism does allow freedom of choice and enables people in the USA to still believe in "the American Dream".

Of course, an upturn in the economic cycle means that everyone is happy. There is near full employment, wages and benefits are good, the feel-good factor encourages people to spend. Then the excesses lead to the inevitable downturn and hardship for many, as workers are laid off, there are bankruptcies, and spending comes to a standstill. Somehow, capitalism has survived these turbulent times. Based on this fact, we can now look at investment in a capitalist society.

To begin with, a meeting place was needed for people, companies, and governments wanting capital to meet people and companies with money to invest. This essential meeting place began in the City of London.

Throughout the eighteenth century, stocks and shares were traded in City of London coffee houses, the most famous being Jonathan's. Business boomed, and then, at the beginning of the second decade, the British government had become almost bankrupt. They needed a large amount of cash and obtained it by selling £9 million of government stock with an attractive rate of interest to a group of financiers who had formed a company called the South Sea Trading Company. Some of you may have read about the ensuing problems which created the first catastrophic company collapse. It was known as "the South Sea Bubble". A recent example of this was the more widespread dot.com bubble.

The South Sea Company owners reckoned that with the government's help in granting them special trading rights in South America, they would make a fortune; they convinced a huge number of investors that they should participate in this bonanza. They sold shares in the company to all and sundry. The faster the share price went up, the more investors were sucked in. Of course, it could not continue, and as with many such schemes, it all came to an end in late 1720. As always, the share price fell faster than it had risen; in fact, it collapsed in a few weeks.

Because of this, the traders of the Jonathan's coffee house decided it was time to form a club to conduct their business. In 1793, the business was moved to a purpose built building. Some members were jobbers and others were brokers. A number of rules and regulations were instituted, and the members named their club The London Stock Exchange.

On 3 March 1801, the business reopened under a formal membership basis with strict regulations. This was the beginning of the modern stock exchange.

In 1836, provincial exchanges opened in Manchester and Liverpool and were followed later by Birmingham, Glasgow, Belfast, and the Channel Islands.

In 1923, the exchange was granted a coat of arms with the motto "*Dictum Meum Pactum*" (My Word Is My Bond).

During World War II, the exchange was closed for six days at the outset in September 1939, and for one day in 1945 due to damage from a German V2 rocket.

I became a member of the Provincial Brokers Stock Exchange (PBSE) in 1972, having passed the PBSE entrance examination. It is interesting to note that members of the London Stock Exchange never had to pass an exam. They considered themselves better educated and more privileged, so it was not necessary for them to have to pass an exam (I think many of them would have found it very difficult to pass our exam).

As a matter of academic interest, our partnership in 1972 turned themselves into the first limited corporate member of the stock exchange. I became a director as opposed to a partner. We took in three outside shareholders: NM Rothschild (CI) Ltd., Hambros Guernsey Ltd., and ICFC Guernsey Ltd.

My office also had the distinction of appointing the first female office manager. When she attended the next Office Managers'

Association dinner in London, the old members thought she had come into the dining hall by mistake.

You may wonder why the stock exchange, the stock market, and stockbrokers are so named, when they actually deal in shares. The answer is that a company is formed with an initial capital of stock, say £100,000, divided into shares of, say, 10p. Thus there would be 1,000,000 shares in issue. These are then bought and sold on the stock market, because they are in effect a share of the issued stock.

It is also important to realise that at this time, there were two types of members of the stock exchange. There were stock jobbers, who made buying and selling prices in stocks to the stockbrokers, who in turn acted on behalf of their clients in buying and selling shares.

In the early 1980s, the Thatcher government, under pressure from the big banks and other institutions such as pension funds, insurance companies, and unit trusts, threatened to abolish the monopoly of the stock exchange. At that time, the members of the "club", as they were known, effectively charged two lots of commission because of the division between jobbers and brokers. The big city institutions objected to this and wanted to become members of the stock exchange and allow "dual capacity": that is to say, they could be market makers and brokers.

The stock exchange members resisted the government's threat for some time and incurred huge legal costs.

In the end, the chairman of the stock exchange, Nicholas Goodison, and the government trade secretary, Cecil Parkinson, did a deal (incidentally, without allowing members to vote for or against it).

On 27 October 1986, the City of London was changed forever. To begin with, there were mergers between banks, brokers, and jobbers. I wrote a paper for my co-directors on the implications of this "Big Bang", and as a direct result of this, Trevor Matthews & Carey Ltd. was sold to Hoare Govett, one of the largest UK stockbrokers. In turn, it had been sold to Securities Pacific, a large American bank on the West Coast.

It took several years for the new players in the London capital markets to settle down. There were good points and bad points. Obviously, the biggest gain was for London to become the world's biggest financial centre, competing with New York. The influx of overseas banks assured its success.

One big downside in my opinion was the abolition of the Stock Exchange Compensation Fund. This was used to fully compensate any investor who lost money dealing with a member who defaulted, due to fraud or mismanagement. To the best of my knowledge, no investor ever suffered a loss. We as members all contributed to this fund. The government were never called on to assist. Perhaps this was due to the fact that most members stuck to the motto, *Dictum Meum Pactum*.

As I write, the world is in the midst of the worst recession since the one that preceded the Great Depression of the 1930s. Unlike that one, this has crippled nations, especially those who are the weaker members of the Euro Currency Union. In 2011, there were more meetings of the world's finance ministers, bankers, and leaders of the European Union than ever before. Their aim was to maintain the Euro currency at all costs. In one way, they were right because a break-up would have serious consequences all over the world. Au contraire, it might have been better to allow some of the weakest to leave the currency, but remain, like Britain, as members of the European Union. After all, there are now ten out of twenty-seven who still have their own currency.

One of the problems with deregulation was that the financial institutions became so huge, and had such diverse activities, that it became almost impossible to regulate them, especially transactions by hedge funds and the derivative markets. Greed took over. It is hard to convince me that a Collective Debt Obligation could be sold by a reputable Wall Street name to another reputable financial institution without either the seller knowing what he was selling or the buyer making sure that his purchase was sound. Had they never heard of "caveat emptor" (buyer beware)? The reason was that the individual dealers' bonuses were paid on turnover. In a way, it was like the old game of pass the parcel. When the music stopped, the holder lost out.

I believe that the music will start again, and the same participants will be passing new parcels. If not, why are their bonuses still so high? The parcels are possibly sovereign debt issues.

There has to be some more regulation, or we might have another crash that would make the one in 2008 look insignificant.

As capitalists, we must assume that our system will survive these downturns. New entrepreneurs will ensure this continuity, so it is vital that governments do not suffocate growth with high taxes and too much regulation.

Recently, there has been a tendency for governments, spurred on by the media, to attack the wealthy. This is the politics of envy, which could precipitate a downward spiral into left wing socialism. Sadly, if all the wealth was redistributed to the poor, it would not perceptively improve their lot, and the next step would be communism or a dictatorship. Therefore, let's hear it for compassionate conservatism!

Stock exchanges around the world are the engines of capitalism. In the twenty-first century, they continue to provide the meeting place for businesses and capital that started with Jonathan's coffee house in the City of London nearly two centuries ago.

Sometimes, the stock exchanges are called casinos, and to the anti-capitalists, they only exist for the rich to become richer. There is of course a great deal of speculative action, but underlying that, the original objects are still flourishing and have enabled brilliant entrepreneurs like Bill Gates, the founder of Microsoft, to build hugely successful businesses, giving employment to thousands of people.

Governments have set dangerous precedents in bailing out private banks and in compensating deposit account holders.

Where it will all end, no one knows. However, the purpose of this book is to guide the reader through the financial jungle with the aim of providing the means of creating an investment plan to provide an income for life in retirement.

Before exploring the types of assets that are dealt in on a stock exchange, I want to briefly touch on the subject of one's own business.

Starting a Business

No book on investing would be complete without a chapter on the idea of starting up one's own business.

There are many reasons for wanting to do this. In the early part of the twentieth century, Britain was called "the nation of shopkeepers", as so many people saw this as an opportunity to work for themselves rather than for a big company. Another major area for small businesses was the building trade. Competent tradesmen thought they would be better off financially by setting up on their own. Shop keeping has been made virtually impossible by the supermarkets, who operate out of town centres with large car parks. The town centre businesses are on the decline, as parking is a huge problem. The building trade, however, is flourishing, and many tradesmen have carved out a lucrative career for themselves. Many would-be entrepreneurs, however, have failed because they did not have any business training. They may be excellent tradesmen, but that is only half the story.

There are many reasons for business failure, but the most likely one is due to being undercapitalised. Another reason for failure is the lack of understanding basic principles such as the need to set budgets.

There are other extraneous reasons over which the businessman has little control, such as economic downturns leading to recession. This hits many businesses, especially the building trade.

Let us make no mistake: starting any business is a commitment that only a few brave individuals will undertake. It is much easier to work a forty-hour week, have a regular income to cover living costs, have three weeks or more paid holiday per annum, and possibly a company pension scheme and health plan.

Why on earth would any sensible person throw these gifts away to work for themselves? The answer I believe is the need for a challenge. Some people meet this need by climbing mountains, skydiving, or spelunking. They want to defeat the odds of achieving their particular goals. So it is with the individual who is bored with the nine-to-five routine.

The easiest business to start is an extension of one's current occupation, such as a tradesman or professional person. Whatever it may be, there is a need for anyone from any background to make some serious assessments of the likely income and the likely costs of their projected venture. They will need to have drive and ambition and be prepared to work for many more hours in the week initially. Over time, they may afford some luxuries that they could never have had from their secure employment. I say why not? They have worked hard for it and given employment to many other people, so they should indulge themselves.

So, where to start? Well, you may have sufficient savings to tide you over for a while, but you will almost certainly need to have an overdraft facility from your bank. This gives you some working capital. Not only that, but the bank will discipline you by asking you to prepare a business plan for three years or more.

It is imperative that you really strive to present an accurate picture; do not be tempted to present an overoptimistic one in the hope that this will make the bank happy to lend. They are not stupid and will have a pretty shrewd idea of what your business is likely to achieve, especially if they already have customers with similar businesses.

In preparing your plan as a tradesman, you should have some idea of how much you can earn in an hour. Multiply this by ten and then by six. That as a sole tradesman is what you can earn in a six-day week. Out of this, you have to pay for an office, a workshop, a van, insurance, a subscription to a trade organisation, printed notepaper, bookkeeping, and so on. You may have no customers, in which case you will have to have a high advertising budget. If you are sensible, you will not start up without knowing that you have some set contract work lined up.

Your business plan is accepted by the bank, so you are ready to start.

Assuming you are successful and find you are obtaining more work than you can cope with, you may need to consider employing another tradesman. This presents a problem. You probably started your business as a sole trader. Now you have to consider whether to take the new person on as a partner or as an employee. If the latter, then you should consider forming a limited company. There are additional costs involved, but you will have protected yourself to some extent by limiting your liability.

If the new person is an employee or a partner, it is unlikely you will have enough work to keep them fully employed initially, which means your profit will fall back until such time as he is fully employed and you will be making a profit on his work.

With each change, you may need to discuss with your bank the need for further overdraft facilities or a loan if, for instance, you need a premises or expensive piece of equipment.

If you keep to your budget, ensure that your invoicing is done promptly, and overdue accounts are chased, everything will be fine.

The most important element of success is to manage your cash flow. Never mind about profits, they will materialise, but seriously monitor cash flow. By this, I mean ensuring that the monthly income matches outgoings. Variations have to be covered by the overdraft facility. If you know that you have made an exceptional purchase which will temporarily mean exceeding your current overdraft limit, contact your bankers and explain it to them. Usually they will appreciate the fact that you have contacted them and allow you the temporary extension to your overdraft facility. If you do not tell them, they are likely to be very difficult, and I would not blame them.

Success of the business is dependent on maintaining a close and open relationship with its sponsors, whether it be a bank or other source of capital.

There are many different businesses that people start up, but the rules are basically the same. As the business develops, there will be new problems to solve. Should you rent or buy the property that you conduct your business from? Returning to the chapter on Property Investment, you will see what I said as far as your own home is concerned: why give the rent to the landlord for him to benefit from?

As far as a business is concerned, however, there are other considerations. It may be more beneficial to increase the stock or employ more sales personnel, and buying a property is really an investment rather than using money to increase turnover and profit. Nevertheless, most successful businesses will at some time hold some real estate.

If you want to go into business but want to avoid the hassle and risk of starting up on your own, you could buy an existing business. You could then decide to buy one with a guaranteed profit, or should I say one that has shown consistent profit for the past five years. This might be a business that has minimum chance of expansion but will give you an acceptable return on your investment.

Better still, of course, would be to buy one where, with your flair, you perceive a great opportunity for expansion.

Valuing smaller unquoted companies is always very difficult. Nearly always the sellers have an inflated view of what it is worth. How much of the business is due to the personal connections of the sellers? Would their customers stay with you as the new owner? This is known as good will and is over and above the physical asset value.

The eventual purchase price is very often based on x times the annual profits. The two times I have bought an existing business, they were run down but capable of being turned round. They ended up being successful businesses, and I sold one at a substantial profit.

As a business grows, it is important to delegate responsibilities to trusted employees so that you have time to plan the future development of your business. For example, if you are better at administration than sales, then employee a good salesperson, and vice versa.

You should always have a good firm of accountants to audit your books and give you tax advice. The latter is of paramount importance, because taxation changes from budget to budget and even more so from government to government. You do not have the time or the expertise to cope with these changes, but your accountants' success depends on their knowledge and competence in the field of taxation.

When you have reached the point where you are making good profits, you can then plan how to use them to further your business. You must have some in a reserve for vital maintenance or replacement of vehicles and equipment used in your business, as nothing lasts forever. You can plan to open new branches or expand by buying out a competitor. There are too many options to elaborate on in this chapter, and success in any type of business is down to drive, ambition, close control over cash flow, and maintaining good relationships with one's bankers. One other asset is being able to select good staff and delegate. Good staff should be rewarded well. Always remember that we all have to work for a living, whether we like it or not, so be respectful and generous to your staff, and you will be rewarded by their respect and loyalty.

Deposits and Treasury Stocks

Investment can take many forms, but eventually, it is how we deal with our excess income and capital distributions that we might receive, such as an inheritance. Our aim is to provide an adequate income on retirement. There are many options open to us, so it is essential to examine them in detail.

The simplest is to open a deposit account with a bank, building society, or other deposit taking institution. Your deposit will produce interest which may be payable monthly or annually. Providing you place it with an institution that is covered by a government guarantee such as the FDIC in America or other scheme in the case of the UK, your deposit will be reimbursed to you by the government should the institution default. There is an upper limit (currently $250,000 in the USA and £85,000 in the UK). Always check to be sure, as these amounts are subject to change. This applies to one institution, so you can spread your risk and have up to £85,000 in several institutions in the UK and be covered for each of them, providing they are not in any way connected with each other.

Interest on these deposits varies according to the amount and the length of time (the term) of your deposit.

Normal deposit accounts are either for instant access or term deposits. The latter can be fixed for set periods of time, from one month to one or more years. Some cannot be broken and others only with penalties, so make sure you will not need the capital before the end of the term.

The only downside to deposits is that you will be unlikely to beat inflation after tax. The length of term that you select is based on the expected movement in interest rates. If they are historically low, you should place your savings on short term deposit because interest rates are eventually expected to rise. When interest rates are historically high, you should place your savings on long term deposit because you expect interest rates to fall.

How do you judge the next move in interest rates? First of all, who sets the interest base rate? It is usually the country's central bank. The central bank's main function is to control inflation. In a deflationary phase, they will set the base rate low to encourage businesses to borrow money to expand. At some point, inflation creeps in; this can be for many reasons. Prices of goods and services rise which leads to demands for higher wages. Higher wages fuel a further rise. Then the central bank will raise the base rate to dampen down the economy.

As I write, interest base rates at 0.5 per cent are as low as they have been for years. This makes forecasting easy because they can in reality only go up. There is still an unknown: when they will start to rise. There is certainly inflation in some areas of the economy, but the recovery from the severe recession is not as robust as the governments would like, and they fear that a rise in interest rates could very easily stop the recovery in its tracks.

Nevertheless, rates will rise eventually. So it is time to keep your term deposits short, say a maximum of twelve months.

Your deposit is not an investment. It is in fact a loan to the bank or financial institution that you have given it to, so it is sensible to lend it to a reputable institution, even if its rates are lower than other outlets. Always remember that there are good reasons why some rates are higher. The higher the rate, the higher the risk.

Can we lend our money any other way? Yes we can, in any number of ways.

Governments, corporations, and municipalities all borrow money. They do this by way of issuing fixed interest loan stocks which you can buy from your bank or stockbroker as they are traded on a stock exchange. These stocks all have a fixed rate of interest for a fixed period; most make interest payments twice a year.

If someone you know asks you for a loan which he guarantees to pay back by a certain date, you would ask yourself, "Do I believe he will pay me back?" Some people would be safer to lend money to than others.

The same applies in the fixed interest market. The safest bet normally would be government stocks known as Treasuries (known colloquially in the UK as Gilts, because they are supposedly gilt edged and 100 per cent safe).

Corporate loan stocks are only as good as the company borrowing your money. Municipals again are only as good as the borrower. Nearly all these loans are rated by a rating agency such as Moody's, S&P, or Fitch. AAA is the highest rating.

Because Treasury loans are issued by a government, they are considered the safest, but would you want to invest in a small country? Recent events with countries within the European Union have shown that it can be risky. Although unlikely to default, the difference between the strongest and weakest countries can mean a big difference in the yields on their loan stocks (or sovereign debt, as their borrowings are called). So you need to look at the ratings; if a yield is above average, ask yourself, why? The higher the reward, the greater the risk, and that applies to all sectors of the fixed interest market.

Loan stocks have a rate of interest set at the time of issue for a fixed period of time and have a par value of 100. That means on redemption at the end of the fixed period of time, the lender will receive 100 per 100 units of stock. During the term of the loan, the price will move up or down, mainly due to movement in base rates set by the central bank.

Treasury stocks are the safest investment and, because of the size of the issues, are used by pension funds and insurance companies, who themselves have large sums of cash to invest from contributions and premium income. Countries with large balance of payment surpluses invariably invest in the Treasury stocks of the country that they have sold goods to. A prime example is China and the USA. That aside, you as an individual can invest your hard-earned savings in Treasury and other fixed interest stocks. Before doing so, it is important to understand some basic facts.

The first is that the central bank sets a base rate. This is a rate on which all other rates are based. For example, if you go to your bank for a loan, they will quote you a rate of x per cent over base. They will also quote you rates for deposits, which will be close to the base rate.

All government corporations and other borrowers will base the rate of interest on their new loans around the central bank's base rate.

The following are samples of the UK Gilt list and the Sterling Bond list, dated 3 August 2012 (copied from Internet site www.bondscape.net).

Gilt closing prices for 03-Aug-2012

epic	description	coupon	maturity	bid	ask	change	income yield	gross redemption yield
CN4	Uk Gilt Consols	4.0	Perpetual	92.02	104.02	-2.02	4.08	4.08 *
WAR	Uk Gilt War Loan Stk	3.5	Perpetual	90.06	100.06	-2.18	3.68	3.68 *
CV3H	Uk Gilt Conversion Stk	3.5	Perpetual	89.81	98.81	-2.00	3.71	3.71 *
T3UD	Uk Gilt Treasury Stk	3.0	Perpetual	73.52	81.76	-0.63	3.86	3.86 *
CN2H	Uk Gilt Consols	2.5	Perpetual	59.49	68.71	-0.56	3.90	3.92 *
T2H	Uk Gilt Treasury Stk	2.5	Perpetual	63.56	71.58	-0.58	3.70	3.70 *
	Uk Gilt Treasury Stk	4.25	07-Mar-2011	100.08	100.13	0.00	0.00	0.00
	Uk Gilt Treasury Stk	3.25	07-Dec-2011	101.33	101.53	0.00	0.00	0.00
TY12	Uk Gilt Treasury Stk	9.0	06-Aug-2012	98.75	101.75	0.00	0.00	0.00
TR13	Uk Gilt Treasury Stk	4.5	07-Mar-2013	102.48	102.58	-0.05	4.39	0.19
T813	Uk Gilt Treasury Stk	8.0	27-Sep-2013	108.94	109.09	-0.09	7.34	0.09
TR14	Uk Gilt Treasury Stk	2.25	07-Mar-2014	103.33	103.48	-0.08	2.18	0.10
T514	Uk Gilt Treasury Stk	5.0	07-Sep-2014	110.15	110.30	-0.10	4.54	0.09
TR15	Uk Gilt Treasury Stk	2.75	22-Jan-2015	106.31	106.46	-0.07	2.58	0.15
T4T	Uk Gilt Treasury Stk	4.75	07-Sep-2015	114.21	114.26	-0.07	4.16	0.13
TY8	Uk Gilt Treasury Stk	8.0	07-Dec-2015	126.17	126.23	-0.12	6.34	0.13
TS16	Uk Gilt Treasury Stk	2.0	22-Jan-2016	105.79	105.89	-0.09	1.89	0.30
T16	Uk Gilt Treasury Stk	4.0	07-Sep-2016	114.65	114.77	-0.17	3.49	0.37
TR17	Uk Gilt Treasury Stk	8.75	25-Aug-2017	140.78	140.76	-0.21	6.22	0.56
T18	Uk Gilt Treasury Stk	5.0	07-Mar-2018	123.58	123.58	-0.23	4.05	0.69
T19	Uk Gilt Treasury Stk	4.5	07-Mar-2019	123.35	123.11	-0.24	3.65	0.86
TR19	Uk Gilt Treasury Stk	3.75	07-Sep-2019	118.33	118.53	-0.39	3.17	1.05
TS20	Uk Gilt Treasury Stk	4.75	07-Mar-2020	126.00	126.19	-0.48	3.77	1.15
TR20	Uk Gilt Treasury Stk	3.75	07-Sep-2020	118.83	119.08	-0.89	3.15	1.28
TR21	Uk Gilt Treasury Stk	8.0	07-Jun-2021	155.26	156.02	-0.47	5.14	1.31
TY21	Uk Gilt Treasury Stk	3.75	07-Sep-2021	119.87	119.43	-0.72	3.13	1.44
TR22	Uk Gilt Treasury Stk	4.0	07-Mar-2022	122.27	121.87	-0.44	3.28	1.52
TR25	Uk Gilt Treasury Stk	5.0	07-Mar-2025	134.80	134.65	-0.61	3.71	1.89
TR27	Uk Gilt Treasury Stk	4.25	07-Dec-2027	127.22	127.13	-0.20	3.34	2.16
TR28	Uk Gilt Treasury Stk	6.0	07-Dec-2028	152.59	152.09	-0.56	3.94	2.18
TR30	Uk Gilt Treasury Stk	4.75	07-Dec-2030	135.29	134.60	-0.34	3.52	2.39
TR32	Uk Gilt Treasury Stk	4.25	07-Jun-2032	127.25	126.66	-0.27	3.35	2.52
T34	Uk Gilt Treasury Stk	4.5	07-Sep-2034	130.63	130.10	-0.42	3.45	2.67
T4Q	Uk Gilt Treasury Stk	4.25	07-Mar-2036	126.10	125.48	-0.50	3.38	2.76
TR38	Uk Gilt Treasury Stk	4.75	07-Dec-2038	135.81	135.05	-0.57	3.51	2.83
T39	Uk Gilt Treasury Stk	4.25	07-Sep-2039	126.00	125.61	-0.35	3.38	2.87
T40	Uk Gilt Treasury Stk	4.25	07-Dec-2040	125.99	125.25	-0.51	3.38	2.92
T42	Uk Gilt Treasury Stk	4.5	07-Dec-2042	131.88	130.98	-0.53	3.42	2.93
T46	Uk Gilt Treasury Stk	4.25	07-Dec-2046	126.83	126.02	-0.67	3.36	3.01
T49	Uk Gilt Treasury Stk	4.25	07-Dec-2049	126.65	125.85	-0.70	3.37	3.06
TR4Q	Uk Gilt Treasury Stk	4.25	07-Dec-2055	128.24	127.25	-0.75	3.33	3.08
TR60	Uk Gilt Treasury Stk	4.0	22-Jan-2060	123.29	122.34	-0.74	3.26	3.08

Note from the list there are three types of Gilts. It starts with the undated or *perpetual* ones; these take no notice of *EPIC* (the stocks on the Stock Exchange EPIC system).

The first item is the *description*, then the *coupon*. This is the rate of interest that was fixed at the time the stock was issued and what will be paid out by way of interest payment in a twelve-month period, based on the par value or, as it is called, the nominal value of 100.

The next column is the *maturity date*, but the first six on the list are perpetual, so look down to the Treasury 4.5 per cent, where the maturity date is shown as 7 March 2013.

The next items are the *bid* and *asking prices*. These are the prices for selling and buying, respectively. The difference between them is the market makers' "turn" on gross profits. Prices change all the time the trading period is on, and the prices shown are not accurate but give an indication. The *change* is the change from the previous day.

The *income or flat yield* is straightforward and is calculated by the following formula:

$$\frac{\text{Coupon}}{\text{Price}} \times 100 = \text{yield}$$

To show this, simply assume the coupon is 5 per cent and the price is 100. Doing your sum, the flat yield is 5 per cent. If the price was higher at 125, the yield would be lower at 4 per cent, and if the price was lower at 90, the yield would be 5.55 per cent.

The point to remember here is that whatever the yield is at the price you pay, you will receive that yield on your investment until the stock is redeemed.

The final figure is *Gross Redemption Yield* (also *Yield to Maturity [YTM]* or *Gross Yield to Redemption [GYR]*). This is the total return on your investment, allowing for the fact that you paid more or less than 100. The calculation is complicated but to explain it in simple terms, if your 5 per cent stock above was due for redemption in five years' time and you paid 115 for it, your flat yield would be 4.4 per cent, but because you are losing 10 points over five years, the YTM would be only about 2.4 per cent.

If you paid 90 for it, your flat yield would be 5.55 per cent but you would have a 10 point gain over five years, so the YTM would be around 7.55 per cent.

Returning to the Gilt List, you will see sizeable differences in the flat yields due to the difference in the coupon. The coupons vary because the stocks are issued at different times in the interest rate cycle, and the government has to issue them at the going rate.

However, the Yield to Maturity or Gross Yield to Redemption take account of this and show yield rising steadily with length of time to redemption.

Euro Sterling closing prices for 03-Aug-2012

epic	description	coupon	maturity	bid	ask	change	income yield	gross redemption yield
EHS5	Hsbc Capital Funding l.p	8.208	Perpetual	102.85	108.85	0.15	7.75	5.85 *
EA26	Abbey National Plc	7.037	Perpetual	83.60	83.60	-0.60	9.56	10.55 *
ESC6	Standard Chartered Bank	8.103	Perpetual	104.95	110.95	-0.25	7.51	5.00 *
	General Elec Cap Corp	6.125	17-May-2012	97.50	102.50	0.00	0.00	0.00
	Tate & Lyle Intl Finance	6.5	28-Jun-2012	99.00	101.00	0.00	0.00	0.00
ECW1	Cable And Wireless Plc	8.75	06-Aug-2012	98.45	101.95	0.00	0.00	0.00
EGN2	GE Capital Uk Funding	5.875	01-Nov-2012	98.65	103.65	0.00	5.81	0.87
ECE2	Centrica PLC	5.875	02-Nov-2012	99.55	102.55	0.00	5.81	1.33
EDX2	Dixons Group Plc	6.125	15-Nov-2012	99.45	101.95	-0.05	6.08	3.36
EK12	KFW	4.75	07-Dec-2012	101.00	101.90	0.00	4.68	0.35
EKM2	Kommunalbanken AS	4.875	10-Dec-2012	99.40	104.40	-0.05	4.78	-0.70
ECF2	Carrefour Sa	5.375	19-Dec-2012	99.90	102.90	0.00	5.30	1.45
EE13	European Investment Bank	4.5	14-Jan-2013	100.20	103.20	-0.05	4.42	0.56
EKW3	KFW	4.875	15-Jan-2013	101.15	102.65	0.00	4.78	0.51
EWM3	Wal-mart Stores	4.75	29-Jan-2013	100.70	103.20	-0.05	4.66	0.63
ET13	Total Capital SA	5.5	29-Jan-2013	100.30	104.30	0.00	5.38	0.63
EGL3	JTI (UK) Finance PLC	5.75	06-Feb-2013	101.00	104.00	0.15	5.61	0.69
ERF3	Eurofima	4.375	11-Feb-2013	99.25	104.25	-0.05	4.30	0.91
EC13	Carlsberg-tuborg A/s	7.0	26-Feb-2013	101.30	104.30	-0.05	6.81	1.80
EG63	GE Capital Uk Funding	6.0	11-Apr-2013	100.85	105.85	-0.05	5.81	0.98
ECB3	CIBA UK Plc	6.5	24-Apr-2013	101.65	104.65	-0.05	6.30	1.97
ER13	RWE Finance Bv	6.375	03-Jun-2013	102.60	105.80	-0.05	6.11	1.07
ED13	Deutsche Telekom Int Fin Bv	5.625	19-Jul-2013	102.50	105.50	-0.05	5.41	1.34
ENX3	Next Plc	5.25	30-Sep-2013	102.30	105.30	-0.05	5.06	1.85
EMS3	Morgan Stanley & Co Inc	5.375	14-Nov-2013	100.30	105.07	-0.02	5.23	3.19
EBA3	BAT Intl Finance Plc	5.75	09-Dec-2013	104.65	107.65	-0.10	5.42	1.08
EG13	General Elec Cap Corp	5.25	10-Dec-2013	103.00	108.00	-0.10	4.98	1.08
EB13	Bank Nederlandse Gemeenten	2.625	10-Dec-2013	101.05	104.05	-0.10	2.56	0.70
EN13	Neder Waterschapsbank	2.375	10-Dec-2013	99.90	103.90	-0.05	2.33	0.94
EGU3	Experian Finance PLC	5.625	12-Dec-2013	104.40	106.90	0.15	5.32	1.34
EW14	World Bank	5.375	15-Jan-2014	105.75	108.75	-0.05	5.01	0.31
EH14	Halifax Plc	11.0	17-Jan-2014	106.97	112.15	-0.03	10.04	3.97
EJL4	John Lewis Plc	10.5	23-Jan-2014	110.75	113.75	-0.10	9.35	1.86
EK14	Kreditanstalt fuer Wiederaufbau	5.375	29-Jan-2014	106.35	107.85	-0.10	5.02	0.53
EK34	KFW	3.25	24-Feb-2014	103.30	105.30	-0.10	3.12	0.45
EMS4	Marks & Spencer Plc	5.625	24-Mar-2014	104.95	106.95	-0.10	5.31	1.86
EE14	European Investment Bank	6.25	15-Apr-2014	107.60	110.60	-0.10	5.73	0.79
EIT4	Italy (Republic of)	10.5	28-Apr-2014	101.80	116.80	-0.05	9.61	4.67
EL14	Lloyds Tsb Bank Plc	5.875	20-Jun-2014	102.20	105.45	-0.10	5.66	3.67
EBR4	European Bk Recon & Dev	5.875	04-Aug-2014	109.05	112.05	-0.10	5.31	0.53

I have also shown one page of the Euro Sterling issues. These are sterling loans issued by corporations and banks. The headings are the same but there is one major difference. Under the *Gross Redemption Yield* column, you will see that there is no correlation according to maturity date. The reason for this is that all Treasuries are issued by one issuer, whereas there are many different companies and banks on the list. They are not all rated as safe as each other, so for example, the 6.25 per cent European Investment Bank 2014 has a much higher rating than the 10½ per cent Italy (Republic of) 2014, and the risk is reflected in their 0.79 to 4.67 Yields to Redemption.

There are also several municipal loans which again are rated according to their risk.

In addition to redeemable fixed interest, there are stocks with a fixed rate of interest but no redemption date. The largest government issue is the 3½ per cent War Loan. Nongovernment issues are known as Permanent Interest Bearing loans (PIBs). Their prices move up or down, mainly with changes in interest rates, but they can also move downwards if the underlying company falls on hard times. They generally yield more than the longer dated redeemable issues.

There are also Index Linked Government Stocks. As their name suggests, these offer investors a prospect of obtaining a real return. They were originally introduced for pension funds but are now available to anyone. They are, however, complex issues and not often bought by private investors. Anyone who is interested in them can read all about them on the UK Debt Management office website.

As with deposits, where you are lending your money to a bank, when you invest in the Gilt and Fixed Interest markets, you should check current base rates and assess the likelihood of change. If they are low with a possibility of rising, then it is best to wait a while until they have risen to a point where you think the next move will be down. That is a good time to look into good rates of interest and prospects of capital appreciation in the medium to long term issues.

The principles of these two forms of investment are the same wherever you live. Although they are referred to as investments, in reality you have just loaned a government or corporation your hard-earned money, which in my book is not a real investment.

There is another type of loan stock known as a Convertible Unsecured Loan Stock. This hybrid stock is issued by corporations rather than governments.

It is a hybrid because in addition to being a loan stock, it can be converted into ordinary shares at some time in the future.

The terms vary from stock to stock, and I personally am not keen on them. I would rather buy a straight loan stock or the ordinary shares in the company. This leads conveniently on to my next chapter.

Stock Exchange Investment

Finally, we have arrived at the point where we can consider investing in the stock market, the object being to build up a sufficient capital sum to provide a major part of our retirement income.

We have done our homework and have a basic knowledge of different types of political systems. We have examined the four stages of economics and should have at least mastered the first.

We understand the principles of capitalism and learned how stock exchanges are a vital part of capitalist societies. We have looked at deposits, Treasury stocks, and other fixed interest stocks. We have looked at the pros and cons of buying one's own property versus renting and by now have reached a decision as to which way to go. So to begin with, we need to understand how to invest and what to invest in.

At this point, I must tell you that there is no tax advice given in this book. You may ask why not, as it is such an important aspect of investment. The answer is that taxation varies from country to country and from individual to individual. Not only that, but the rules and regulations can be changed by governments when they announce their annual budgets. You should always speak to a tax accountant to give you guidance as to the current tax situation and how it might affect your investment decisions.

For instance, many countries offer tax-efficient savings schemes. They are essentially vehicles within which the income builds up tax free, and there are no taxes on capital gains. These plans should be investigated thoroughly before committing, as they have some hidden drawbacks. Although there is no income tax, there is a management fee, which can be 1 per cent per annum based on assets. If there was a tax of 20 per cent on income, it might not be as much as the 1 per cent fee.

To illustrate this, I have assumed investing £100,000 with a gross income of £4,000 per annum:

	Outside Scheme		Inside Scheme
Capital	100,000	Capital	100,000
Gross Income	4,000	Gross Income	4,000
	104,000		104,000
Tax at 20%	800	Fee 1%	1,000
Net position	103,200	Net position	103,000

Just check all these fees, charges, and taxes, in or out of the vehicle. You are allowed to make some capital gains every year tax free in the UK, and it may well be about the same as you make in the vehicle, so there is no advantage there either. It is really a question of personal tax liabilities; you should be sure to do the sums before committing to these schemes.

Irrespective of whether you use such a vehicle, you will need to learn about investment in the stock market.

Having decided to take the plunge and make a start, how to go about it? You may think that the stock market is only for the rich and that your small savings will be of no interest to an investment manager. Absolutely wrong! For a start, any pension scheme you contribute to will have invested your contributions into the stock market.

As an individual investor, you have many options open to you, either by dealing direct with a fund manager of a unit trust/mutual fund, using the services of an intermediary such as a bank or financial adviser, or dealing with a stockbroker.

Before deciding on which of these options to use, it is important to learn about some investment vehicles that are widely promoted for the smaller investor.

Collective Investment Vehicles

There are four main types. The original ones in the UK were known as investment trusts, then came unit trusts (known as mutual funds in the USA. They were followed by Open-Ended Investment Companies (OEICs).

There are substantial differences between the vehicles, and it is very important to understand them.

Investment trusts are limited companies with shares. Their shares are dealt in and quoted on a stock exchange, just like thousands of other companies. They have a board of directors who appoint an investment manager to make investment decisions on their behalf.

When such a company is formed, it issues a prospectus detailing its objectives and how much capital it plans to raise. The public are invited to apply for these new shares. The issue is nearly always "underwritten". This term means that one or more financial institutions have guaranteed to take up the balance of the shares being issued in case the public fail to apply for them all. This way, the directors are certain to raise all the capital they want. This is then invested according to the parameters set out in the offer document. Very often, an investment trust specialises in a geographical area or a particular section of the stock market.

If the investment trust's investment advisers are good at their job, the assets of the company rise, causing the shares to rise. Sometimes, the share price exceeds the underlying asset value. This would occur, for instance, if the trust was so successful that there were more buyers than sellers of the shares. More often, the shares of an investment trust stand at a price lower than the underlying asset value of the share. This is called a discount. If the market that the investment trust invests in suffers a drop, there may be more sellers than buyers, which will widen the discount.

It is therefore wise when buying to (a) be sure the investment trust invests in an area you want to be in, and (b) check the amount of the discount and see whether it is more or less than the average.

After a fall in the market, the discount often widens, so buying shares at that point can give you a double lift when markets improve, as the share price will rise with the increase in asset value, and the discount will narrow.

Another big difference is that their directors can have the power to borrow money to invest. This is known as "gearing" or "leveraging". Because the investment trust only has to pay interest on the loans, all the gains above that interest payment go to the shareholders. The value of their shares goes up, and they could also receive a higher dividend. The downside is that if the market falls, the gearing works in reverse, meaning that on top of the capital loss, interest on the loan has to be paid.

All investment trusts, just like any other company, have to hold an annual general meeting (AGM), which all shareholders are entitled to attend. If you have any questions, such as "What are the directors' borrowing powers?" this is the time to put them to the directors. AGMs are mainly formal meetings with simple agendas which only take a short time to get through, but under "Any other business", the chairman might outline some new developments or answer shareholders' questions. Sometimes, they can become very heated; I recommend that you attend some and meet the members of the board of directors who are investing your hard-earned savings.

Sometimes, the directors use a different method of obtaining further funds to invest. This is known as a "Rights Issue". In investment trusts, the purpose of this is to invite shareholders to put in more money for the directors to invest. They would only be able to do this if they had demonstrated that their management was very successful. If this is so, the shareholders might be amenable to investing more money. To incentivise them, these rights are usually offered at a discount to the recent quoted price of the ordinary shares.

If the directors are dubious about the shareholders' willingness to put their hands in their pockets to take up all these rights, they can use a bank or other financial institution to underwrite the issue. This means that in the event that the shareholders do not apply for all the rights, the underwriters take up the balance. This ensures that the amount of capital the directors wished to raise is guaranteed.

I once experienced an unusual Rights Issue. It was underwritten by a particular financial institution but offered at a price above the recent quoted price of the shares. This was in fact a very clever move on the part of the underwriting institution. They wanted to take a significant stake in the company; rather than buying shares in the market in dribs and drabs, because the shares were not frequently traded, they devised this unusual Rights Issue. They were fairly sure that most shareholders would see no merit in paying over the market price for the rights, and therefore most of the shares would fall into their eager hands. They were correct. I have never seen this done before or since.

Investment trusts are often referred to as "closed end funds". This simply means that they have a fixed amount of shares. The shares are therefore subject to supply and demand as well as the real asset value, whereas some of the other trusts I am going to describe are "open ended", because they can expand or contract the number of units in issue (but the units always remain a true percentage of the asset value).

Most people know about *unit trusts/mutual funds*. There are literally hundreds of these funds worldwide, covering every geographical area and most market sectors.

The structure of these vehicles is very different to that of the investment trusts. Unlike shares in investment trusts, which are quoted and dealt in on a stock exchange, unit trusts and mutual funds are formed by a management group, and their units are priced and dealt in by the fund management company. For example, a fund management group decides to launch a fund specialising in UK equities. A prospectus is drawn up and directors appointed. They in turn appoint the fund management company to act as investment advisers. Units rather than shares are issued, and only when there is a demand. A portfolio is built up, and the assets are valued, usually on a daily basis. The asset value is then divided by the number of units in issue to arrive at the price per unit. There is never a discount or premium to the asset value, as there is with shares in an investment trust. Most investors prefer this structure, and that is why there have been very few new investment trusts created recently.

Fund managers have to make money to cover the cost of managing the investments, and their fees are obtained in several ways.

You will hear talk of "front end load" and "no load" funds. This relates to the entry cost to the investor. The maximum front end load is normally 5 per cent, which means that if you put £100 in a fund, only £95 is actually invested. You immediately have lost £5. Spread over a number of years, this becomes less significant.

"No load" means that all your money is invested, but there may be a catch. There could be a penalty imposed when you sell, called a "back end load". The amount usually depends on how long you have held the units.

If you deal in a unit trust or mutual fund, you deal either directly through the fund manager or through an intermediary such as a bank or stockbroker. Sometimes, the front end load will be less using an intermediary, because they receive part of it from the fund managers as a fee for selling their fund. If they, for example, receive 3 per cent out of the 5 per cent, they may charge you only 3 per cent (i.e., 2 per cent for the fund manager and 1 per cent for themselves). It is certainly worth checking, because it is foolish to lose 5 per cent of your investment by dealing direct if you can save 2 per cent by dealing through an intermediary.

The other fees you need to be aware of are performance fees. These give the fund managers a bonus for good performance. You may think this is reasonable, but don't forget their normal annual fee is based on the value of the assets, so if the fund's assets have gone up, they receive an increase anyway. Personally, I think it is their job to perform well, and they should be satisfied with their normal fees. If the fund's assets depreciate, would they reduce their fees? If they don't perform better than their benchmark, they should consider alternative employment.

All these funds carry a wealth warning that stock markets go down as well as up.

Bearing all these points in mind, an investment of this type may be the best way for you to begin investing, as you do not have to personally make any investment decisions. Of course, you do have to make the initial investment, so how do you decide on which fund to invest in?

You should do some research on the Internet or read a publication like *Morningstar*, which rates the performance of different funds. You can ask your bank or speak to a stockbroker or other financial adviser. You can also speak directly with the fund managers, but beware if they recommend all their funds. There is no one fund management group that I know of that has the world's best performing fund in every sector of the market. Unbiased advice is best.

One important point to remember is that when you give an order to buy or sell a unit trust, the price will not be today's price but the price that it is valued at the following day. If the price changes overnight due to some cataclysmic event, you will either get a shock or be overjoyed.

Open-Ended Investment Company or *Open-Ended Investment Vehicle (OEIV)*. These are a mixture between an investment trust, which is a closed-ended vehicle (because it has a fixed share capital), and a unit trust, which expands or contracts the number of units according to buying and selling of the units.

OEICs or OEIVs are managed by fund managers. They have shares, not units, which can be bought or sold at one price, namely the net asset value (NAV). Like unit trusts, there are annual management fees.

All collective investment schemes have the same objective, and that is to make money for the managers and the investors. The better the performance, the more the managers make, as they take a percentage of the NAV, so there is an incentive for them to perform well. Also, they will attract more buyers so they can issue more shares or units and make more money. Investment trusts are different because they are closed ended and do not have this flexibility, which may be the main reason why there are very few of them.

One interesting investment trust is the Investment Trust of Guernsey Ltd. This was originally formed for a very specific reason. Guernsey residents could invest in UK and overseas' equities via a Guernsey company instead of in their own names. This meant that when they died, their estate only held shares in a Guernsey company, on which there would be no inheritance tax, whereas there would have been if they had invested in their own names. Even if there was no liability, the executors would have to deal with every country that the person had invested in, which would have been an expensive exercise.

The advantage of these collective investment vehicles is that you, the investor, do not have to make decisions as to which stocks to buy. You are employing a fund manager to do it on your behalf. Another advantage is that a small capital sum can be diversified. It is also possible to invest by regular monthly instalments in some unit trusts. This has the effect of employing an investment strategy known as "pound cost" (or "dollar cost") averaging. This evens out the fluctuations in the share price, and you do not have the agonising decision to make of when to invest. The basis of the strategy is simply this: each month, you invest the same amount of money. This means you will buy more shares if the price has fallen and fewer shares if the price has gone up. It is a particularly good idea when you are in a position to set aside a small amount of your monthly salary for regular investment.

Passive Investment Vehicles

Passive investments are another important group of investment vehicles.

Index tracker funds were devised to allow investors to invest in an index rather than a share or collection of shares, as in the collective investment vehicles. All these funds mirror the index in which they invest in. For instance, instead of picking and choosing some of the 100 shares that comprise the Financial Times Stock Exchange 100 Share Index, in the hopes of beating the whole, you will always nearly match it. I say "nearly" because the managers of this tracker fund have to make charges, and these come out of the price of the fund.

Exchange traded funds (ETFs) are an extension of the index tracker funds. They offer investors the ability to invest in indices, individual market sectors, commodities, and so on. You can even buy "short" ETFs. They go up in value when the market goes down.

They are traded on a stock exchange and therefore can be dealt in at any time the market is open. Investors can therefore limit their decision making to some extent, by selecting an index or group of similar companies. The other attractions of these funds are their liquidity (ease of dealing), low annual costs, and specificity.

There is one other kind of investment which has recently been available to the smaller investor. *Hedge funds* were once only available to ultra-rich individuals. They aim to give a total return above the market average. These investments are, however, very complex, and they have had a very mixed performance. Some have done incredibly well for their managers and the investors, but most have had a fairly pedestrian performance. It is impossible to compare their performance, because they employ such complex methods. If you are tempted to invest, you need to look for funds with a good five-to ten-year record that consistently returns 8 per cent or more.

Investment in the Stock Market

If you have used a stockbroker for advice on which collective and passive funds to invest in, you will then be ready to expand your portfolio by investing in the shares of an individual company.

The decision may be sparked by observation, by reading in the newspapers, or by seeing something on television. In my case, it was by observation. When I had a business in Dorking, I noticed a shop in the high street of a new company called Tesco. What intrigued me was the food retailer's presentation, and the fact that every time I drove by there were so many customers in the shop. I asked a friend of mine who was a stockbroker if he had heard of the company. He had, and I opened an account with his stockbroking company and made my first purchase-200 Tesco ordinary shares. I sold them 10 years later for a vast profit.

Nearly all national newspapers have a business section which will give prices, daily movements of stock prices, market commentary, and so on.

The only dedicated financial paper in the UK is the *Financial Times*, which is easily distinguishable because it is printed on pink paper (there is also an American edition). The United States has a wide choice of daily papers dedicated to finance, such as the *Wall Street Journal* and the *Investor's Business Daily*. The UK does not have a dedicated financial TV channel, but in America there is CNBC and Bloomberg. If you have never read the *Financial Times,* you may well be bewildered by the amount of information it contains, so I will endeavour to guide you through it.

The Hill of Affluence

There are always some pages dedicated to national and world news. This gives you an idea of what might affect the stock market. A hurricane in the Gulf of Mexico, for instance, will put the price of oil up. A terrorist act in Israel will increase the likelihood of retaliation, risking another Middle East conflict. These days, the media is a 24/7 global operation, so news is disseminated at a very fast rate. This tends to increase volatility in the short term, which can be good for the active traders but a little confusing for investors. That is why pension fund managers indulge in longer term investing.

There are other pages on companies and markets, covering individual company results, currency movements, and market reports. Then you come to the market data pages.

There are details of many currencies, showing their denomination and their value against the US Dollar, the Euro, or the Pound Sterling. It also shows any change in value since the previous day.

There are lists of Global Investment Grade Bonds, Government Benchmark Bonds, High Yield Bonds, and Emerging Market Bonds.

They are by no means complete lists but they do give the reader a good idea of prices (i.e., what yields to expect for bonds of varying maturities).

The Government Benchmark Bonds show how the market views the prospects for a nation's sovereign debt. In August 2012, the ten-year yields showed the US bonds yielding 1.68 per cent, the UK 1.53 per cent, and the Spanish 6.44 per cent. The Greek 11 Year Maturity Bond was yielding a staggering 24.12 per cent. This of course reflects the strong likelihood of a Greek default.

In addition to showing bid prices and yields, the other two categories also show the ratings (triple A being the best) from the three major agencies: Standard and Poor's (S), Moody's (M), and Fitch (F).

There may be a yield curve for the dollar or sterling. This is a graphic way of showing the rate of interest on short to long dated bond maturities. The August 2012 *Financial Times* showed a flat curve for five years, then rising to around 2 per cent in ten years, to

2¾ per cent in thirty years. This gives an indication as to how long the economy is expected to take to recover from recession and low inflation. It can change quite rapidly when inflation returns and interest rates rise. The curve will then rise steeply.

The ten-year government bond spread shows the difference above or below the bond and the T-bond rates and therefore the risk reward ratios.

The Gilts UK FTSE Actuaries Index shows the yields on the various maturities and irredeemables, such as War Loans.

The Gilts UK Cash Market shows the prices, changes, redemption yields, and the fifty-two-week highs and lows for all government issues.

There is a list of commodity prices and various other items such as interest rate swaps and equity options, which are not likely to be of interest to readers of this book.

A separate page lists some larger American stocks, quoted on the New York Stock Exchange and NASDAQ, and international stocks.

The column headings are Price, Change on Day, 52 Week High and Low, Yield, P/E (Price Earnings Ratio), and Volume of Shares Traded.

Also shown are active stocks and the biggest movers, both up and down.

The next page is the Financial Times Share Service. This shows companies traded on the main market, followed by those traded on the Alternative Investment Market. The column headings are the same as for the American market. They change for investment companies.

The first section lists conventional companies, then venture capital trusts. The column headings are the same: Price, Change on Day, High and Low for the Year, Yield, NAV, and finally, Discount or Premium.

For the ordinary income shares, income shares, capital shares and zero dividend preference shares, the column headings are slightly different.

The mechanics of the market are the hardest for the novice to learn about, because they are not mentioned in the media. I will detail some of them here, which can have a bearing on how you invest.

The markets essentially are used by individual investors, corporations such as pension funds and insurance companies, and fund managers of unit and investment trusts. Then there are the speculators such as hedge funds. They make money not by serious investment but by giving long or short of an individual stock or commodity or index. You name it-they do it. These deals can have the effect of artificially changing the price. For instance, you may read that the market went up due to "bear closing".

At this point, I should explain what "shorting" means. If you think that a share or index might fall, you can sell it (even if you do not own it). If you own it, you are a "covered bear" and can deliver the stock to the market on settlement day, but if you don't own it, you are a "naked bear" and have to buy it back. This buying back causes the price to rise. The buying is not a genuine new investment; it is "bear closing" and means that the price will shortly revert back to its previous level.

With this knowledge, you will be ready to converse sensibly with your chosen stockbroker or financial adviser. They will offer you different levels of investment management.

Direct Investment

There are several different methods available for the more adventurous investor who wants to invest directly into individually quoted shares. To my mind, the one most suited to the novice investor is where a broker makes suggestions that suit your investment parameters. It is very important that you specify the income you want from the investments, the level of risk that you wish to bear, and any preference like avoiding tobacco stocks. You should also indicate if you want to diversify some assets into another currency such as the US Dollar or the Euro.

This is an excellent way to learn how to structure a portfolio and the mechanics of the stock market. You can build up a good relationship with your broker over a period of time. Of course, for this service you will be paying their full commission plus fees for holding stock on your behalf. This is where you need to be sure that they have a nominee company which is segregated from their brokerage account. This means that your stocks and cash balances held in their nominee company are safe if the brokerage company defaults. You may earn some interest on the cash balance, but it will not offer an attractive rate. You should therefore only leave cash with the broker that you intend to invest.

The second service they will normally offer is a full discretionary investment service. This is suitable for clients who have no time or interest in making their own investment decisions. It might suit busy professionals, entrepreneurs, or retired people who are planning on travelling around the world.

If you do decide to go down this route, it is vitally important that you tell your discretionary portfolio manager exactly what you want to achieve from your portfolio. Explain as much as possible, including personal details regarding your marital status and your tax position. For instance, if you are comparatively young and plan to work for another ten years, the portfolio can be more aggressive than if you are retired and hope to achieve some capital growth but also need income.

The more you tell your discretionary portfolio manager, the better he or she will be able to perform according to your wishes.

You will receive reports quarterly, half-yearly, or annually, which will show you how the portfolio has performed and what income has arisen over the period, so that your accountant can calculate your income tax and capital gains tax.

When business pressures ease, or when it takes your fancy, you may decide to manage your own investment portfolio. You have two options: one is to stay with your broker and try to negotiate reduced charges (such as a flat x per cent rate of dealing commissions); better still will be to transfer to a dealing only institution. There are several such firms to choose from, and you should compare their charges before opening an account. You also need to compare the services they offer in addition to dealing. They should offer foreign exchange services, multicurrency income earning deposits, free nominee service, and free dividend collections.

Online Stockbroking

For this method, you will need to be computer literate and also understand the various types of dealing order such as "at market", "at limit", or "fill and kill".

"At market" means the best price available in the market now.

"At limit" means you only want to buy or sell at a limit price which can be for one day, one week, one month, and so on.

"Fill and kill" means that you will only deal if the whole of your order can be executed in one deal. You may be trying to deal in a large amount of stock which is way above the normal size in the market. This means that you may only sell part of your holding or buy part of what you want to buy. Because the price is very often adjusted up or down after a large order has been satisfied, you could be faced with several changes in the price every time you deal. This is where a "fill or kill" order is useful. I must admit that I rarely use this option, preferring to deal in stocks whose normal size matches my requirements.

To open an account, you will have to provide the online broker with your full name, current residential address, a certified copy of your passport, and one or two recent utility bills to prove that you are living at the address you have given.

Once these formalities have been completed, the broker will give you a trading account number and password, also a savings account number. There will be a separate dealing account number. In order to access the website, you will have to enter your trading account number and password.

You will then have to experiment with their website to find what you want. Features vary from broker to broker, but you will have access to details of your cash balances, your stock holdings, and your gains and losses (both realised and unrealised). You will also be able to see your entire account history for at least twelve months in all the different currencies that you use.

There will also be extensive research facilities to enable you to select shares that meet your criteria such as income stocks, growth stocks, value stocks, and momentum stocks.

This is therefore an amazing resource that enables you to invest at very low cost. Dealing costs can vary but are usually around £10 a bargain. If you are purchasing a stock with a value of £20,000, the full service broker's charge would be a minimum of £200, so you have saved £190.

The figures in other countries would be similar. It is obviously very attractive for the medium to large private investor.

Then there is the question of the minimum amount of capital that is needed to open such an account. Traditional brokers will normally recommend using collective investment vehicles for capital of £100,000 or higher, some as high as £250,000. The reasons for this are twofold. One is that you need to have a spread of at least twenty individual stocks. The second is that with their high commission charges for buying and selling, it is hard to make a profit on smaller deals.

With online brokers, you can make money on a £1,000 deal if it rises by over 2 per cent, whereas with traditional brokers who generally impose a minimum commission of £100, you would need a rise of over 10 per cent to make money.

In practice, I think a figure of £100,000 with twenty holdings of £5,000 is an ideal minimum for dealing online. It can be much less, of course, if you are going to invest in fewer stocks. Low commissions are of particular importance to active traders, because they can make a profit with a small rise in the price. An investment of £100 with an in-and-out commission of £10 would mean the value of your investment would have to rise 20 per cent just to break even. An investment of £1,000, however, would only have to rise by 2 per cent to break even. There may be other charges to cover, such as stamp duty. It is therefore important to add up all these dealing costs and decide on what your minimum investment should be.

Most stock exchange transactions are for settlement in three business days after the deal. You can deal for a longer date, say, ten business days. The price may change a little, but sometimes it does not. The advantage is that a trader, as opposed to an investor, is able to close the deal within ten days and make a profit without laying out any cash.

The Hill of Affluence

I have previously mentioned "short selling". Not all brokers will accept these deals. If they do, they may require you to place some funds into their account in case your deal goes wrong. Selling means you are a "bear" of the stock, versus buying, which means you are a "bull".

You are known as a "naked bear" or "short seller" when you have no stock to deliver to the market, because you think the price is going to fall. If it does so, well and good because you can buy the shares back, close your position, and pocket the profit.

This can be a dangerous ploy because it can go the other way, and you have to close the position at a loss, which can be substantial. That is why you have to deposit cash with your broker.

Just imagine you sell 100,000 shares of Widgets at 100p per share. The day after you sell, Widgets receives a bid for its shares from another company at a price of 130p per share. To protect yourself against a higher offer or a counter bid, you close your position and lose £30,000. This is an extreme example, but let's say you believe that an oil company drilling off the Nigerian coast is due to report the result of the drilling. You reckon it will be a dry well and the price will collapse. Instead, they announce a new find of a large oil field, and the price goes up instantly. You have to close your short position and obviously lose a lot of money. This where trading is riskier than longer term investment.

It can work the other way too. You may buy a large amount of stock with no intention of paying for them in the next ten days, because you will close the deal by selling. Unfortunately for you, the company announces a dry well and the share price collapses. You close your position and make a loss.

These transactions are best left to gamblers. The same applies to forward deals or dealing in futures. It is a gamble, but it can be an insurance or hedge for some businesses. As an example, you as finance director know that your transport company is going to need to buy 100,000 gallons of diesel fuel in the next six months. You can buy

100,000 gallons for delivery in six months at a fixed price. If the price goes up in the meantime, you will receive a pat on the back from the chairman. If it goes down, you might well get a kick in the pants.

Another version of this market ploy is to deal in traded options. They are quite complicated, and I would not recommend them for the novice investor. Before attempting to invest in them, you should read up on the subject and do some practise deals before you actually lay out your hard-earned cash. They can be useful for the sophisticated investor. It is all a question of give or take for the call or the put. Intrigued? Then read up about them on an Internet site. This book is merely launching you into the world of basic investment, not extending into the more complicated strategies.

How do stockbrokers and financial advisers obtain information on which to base their advice to clients? We will examine these methods in the next chapter.

Research and Analysis

All the larger stockbroking companies employ armies of economists and analysts in their research departments. Their job is to inform the firm's clients about what is happening in their own country and overseas which might have a bearing on their investment opportunities. The economists' job is mainly concerned with the overall picture, whereas the analysts look into individual companies. For instance, economists will listen to the central bank's reports in order to assess the likelihood of a change in interest rates. They will also discuss the economic effect of a huge range of subjects, from a freeze in Florida (affecting the price of orange juice) to the value of the Euro (if one of the Eurozone countries defaulted).

They use statistics, which are of course factual, to emphasise their findings; however, statistics can be arranged in such a manner as to misrepresent the long or short term picture. An investment fund might have performed very well over the past year but underperformed over five years.

The analysts delve into the performance of individual companies. There are two distinct types of analysts, namely technical and fundamental.

The technical analysts believe that the price of any stock reflects everything known about the company.

The price moves up or down whether more investors are buying or selling. These analysts use charts to forecast likely movement in the price based on how the stock price moved in the past. They use various terms to illustrate their theories, such as "head and shoulders", "double bottom", "double top", and "pennant formations".

Fundamental analysts use two distinct methods of evaluation known as quantitative and qualitative analysis. The former, as the name suggests, looks at quantities which, when related to a company, means the figures in its balance sheet and its profit and loss account. From these figures, they apply various ratios to arrive at the intrinsic value of the shares.

In addition to this historic information, they use qualitative analysis, which, as its name suggests, means the quality of a company. They look at the growth in earnings, the dividend record, and the most recent company reports. They note any changes on the board of directors, which might signal different approaches to company strategies and affect the next year's results. Is the company pension fund properly funded? Is there any pending litigation? All these issues help to build up a picture of the quality of the company, which will add to or subtract from its intrinsic value.

The former involves speaking to companies' directors to find out what the position is now and what might happen within the next year. How will changes in government affect their sales? If they are exporters or importers, how will currency movement affect their bottom line, and so on.

The latter is similar to technical analysis in that it relates to known facts and figures and can be churned out by computers.

Both methods have their aficionados. To my mind, chartists' forecasts tend to be self-fulfilling. If a chartist draws lines and suggests because a certain pattern has formed that the price should rise, his or her followers will buy the stock, which will cause the price to rise; therefore, it is self-fulfilling. I look at charts and listen to chartists' recommendations but rely more on the fundamental analysis to make an investment decision. I also believe in reading the latest company reports. The directors, after all, should have the best idea as to what

The Hill of Affluence

the future holds. It is quite noticeable that these reports vary from being realistic to optimistic. One has to remember that even directors cannot always give you an accurate forecast because of the variables. Some reports are deliberately vague because of the variables; others are optimistic, which I like, especially if previous forecasts have been reasonably accurate.

Just to illustrate how difficult it is for anyone to make accurate forecasts, I looked at a recent list of brokers' recommendations for Tesco, which is a large UK food retailer. There were six listed. One was a buy, two were holds, one was a weak sell, and two were sells.

I also looked at Marks & Spencer, which is a UK retailer of food and clothing. The eight recommendations were two buys, six holds, and two sells. I do not know whether the analysts were technical or fundamental or if they used quantitative or qualitative analysis, but I do know that I am totally confused. It proves that analysis is as imprecise an art as is economics and weather forecasting. Like radar to the navigator—purely an aid—so analysis is to the investor. Having said that, you as the ship's navigator or as an investor have to interpret what you see on your screens and use the information to find the best course to steer to avoid the rocks.

There are several terms used by investment analysts that need to be understood, as they are useful in making an assessment of the value and soundness of an individual company.

The first and most used is the P/E (Price to Earnings ratio):

= $\dfrac{\text{Price per Share}}{\text{Earnings per Share}}$

where Earnings per Share = $\dfrac{\text{Net Income}}{\text{Number of Shares outstanding}}$

It shows the number of years for the earnings to equate to the share price. It is therefore used to compare the value of similar companies. Some companies have lower P/E ratios than others, so when people talk about the P/E ratio of an index such as the S&P500 or the FTSE250, it is an average. This average P/E is also a useful guide as to the value of the market. For instance, the P/E ratio of the S&P500 at the end of January 2013 was 14.00, which was below an average of 15.1 for the last decade. The higher the P/E, the greater the risk that the index or share price is overvalued. You will often hear analysts talk about a demanding P/E ratio. It indicates that if the forecast profits are not met, the share price might well fall. It is therefore a very important indicator.

Another useful ratio is the Price to Book ratio:

$$\text{Price to Book ratio} = \frac{\text{Price per Share}}{\text{Book Value per Share}}$$

where

$$\text{Book Value per Share} = \frac{\text{Total Shareholders' Equity}}{\text{Number of Shares}}$$

This shows whether the market price is above or below the book value. It can be used to see whether different companies in the same type of business are expensive or cheap relative to their book values.

$$\text{Current Ratio} = \frac{\text{Current Assets}}{\text{Current Liabilities}}$$

This is used to estimate the solvency of a company in an ongoing situation. If a company was going to be wound up, there is a stricter ratio:

$$\text{Quick Ratio} = \frac{\text{Total Assets minus Stock}}{\text{Total Current Liabilities}}$$

There are numerous other ratios, some being very unreliable, such as the PEG ratio. This is the P/E divided by the growth in earnings over a period of time, which can be historical or anticipated. There are too many uncertainties.

Two other tools you will see are Alpha and Beta. The former is a measurement of risk and should be zero or just above to show that the stock price is at a reasonable level of risk. The latter is a measurement of volatility and should be about one which indicates the stock is about in line with its benchmark. More than one indicates relatively high volatility.

You should also understand some aspects of stock dividends. You need to be sure if the published dividend is gross or net of tax. Sometimes there is a higher rate of tax deducted for non-residents, which may or may not be taxed again in your country of residence. I say this because some entries have double taxation agreements so that only one tax is paid. The net income is what you need to know so that the return on your investment can be compared with other forms of investment.

It is most important to see how many times the dividend payment is covered by taxed earnings. A cover of two times earnings is a good sign. If it is only just covered, there is a risk of the next dividend being reduced if forecast earnings are not forthcoming. Some young growing companies may well retain a substantial part of their earnings for investment. This is perfectly understandable, but if no growth occurs, you need to question why.

All these factors are taken into account by fundamental analysts, and you should certainly try to learn the basics so that you can make your own evaluation. In addition, you should read the news items relating to individual stocks that you are interested in and peruse the latest chairman and directors' reports, especially their forecasts for the following year. This can only be a guide as to the likely outcome, because they cannot foresee external events, which could derail their forecasts.

If you feel that all the work involved in fundamental analysis is not worth the candle, then perhaps you should rely solely on technical analysis.

Whichever method you eventually believe to be the best, you must bear in mind that neither is 100 per cent accurate (or we would all be millionaires).

The "Tilden Theory"

I am writing the last chapter of my book while sitting on the lanai of my winter home in Florida. This was part of my retirement dream. I wanted to spend my last years enjoying life to the fullest. Instead of dull and dreary winter days in Northern Europe, I am able to play golf, swim, and bicycle. I attribute my current good state of health to be a result of this lifestyle, combined with a good set of genes.

The whole object of this book is to encourage and guide you, the reader, to be able to enjoy a lifestyle of your choice when you retire.

We all have different ideas, but the one thought we have in common is to achieve contentment. Set your goals, whatever they may be, and strive to achieve them. To do this, you must avoid the politics of envy.

Imagine you live on a hill. Down in the valley below, lives most of the world's population. As you move up this "hill of affluence", you reach your own position; above you, there are fewer and fewer people. In fact, if you are reading this book, you are already on this hill and well above the valley. I just want you to reach a point where you are content with your lifestyle; do not resent the fact that some people live above you. In fact, their multimillions may make them less content, but the point is you should appreciate the fact that you are where you want to be. Be grateful that you are about 95 per cent of the way to the top and be considerate to the vast bulk of the world's population who live in the valley below you.

I said in my introduction that it is essential for all investors to have a basic knowledge of politics and economics. Now I am going to tell you how to deploy this knowledge when it comes to investment planning.

Politics is most important; that is why I have explained the different systems. The election cycle in America is most relevant, because elections are held every two years for the House of Representatives and one third of the Senate. Every four years, there is a presidential election. This means that electioneering never stops.

President Obama spent a staggering $1.1 billion on his re-election campaign. His opponent, Mitt Romney, spent almost as much.

Raising such vast sums of money implies that the politicians concerned owe something in return to their largest donors.

How does this influence our opinion regarding investment in the American stock market? For a start, I believe every portfolio should have at least 25 per cent of its assets in this market, because it is the only truly capitalist society in the world. Both Democrats and Republicans are capitalists, unlike Europe, where there is a strong socialist influence.

Some industries such as tobacco, oil, and the National Rifle Association (NRA) donate to both parties, so whichever side wins, they hope to have some chance of being heard.

Before explaining the "Tilden theory" of investing for retirement, I want to return to basics. The time is 2013, and I need to assess the current political and economic situation in the USA, the UK, and Europe.

One cannot forget these subjects, especially politics. In a democratic society, we are always preparing for an election or worrying about the aftermath of an election.

The recent elections in America were bitterly fought between the Democrats and the Republicans. President Obama was desperately keen to be re-elected for his second four-year term, spending over $1 billion in the process. He threw such a vast sum of money to win and also had the best technological method of sourcing potential voters. Suffice it to say that he was re-elected with a decisive Electoral College vote. The Senate has a small Democrat minority, but the House of Representatives has a Republican majority. It will be interesting to see how President Obama can win over enough Republicans to enable him to support his political agenda.

Obama has a highly contentious domestic item to deal with: tightening the laws and regulations regarding the sale and ownership of guns, especially automatic weapons, which have been used in recent mass murders. Unlike the UK, Australia, and Japan, which now have very strict controls due to changes in legislation, Americans, under the Second Amendment of the Constitution, have the right to bear arms. This is very strongly supported, especially by the NRA, so it is unlikely that there will be any substantial changes to the existing regulations. Apart from the sensational mass murders, which are usually carried out by deranged men, there are thousands of other deaths by guns every year. The only solution that will overcome this problem while complying with the Second Amendment rights is to strengthen the licensing of all weapons, as is the case in the UK.

As the commander in chief, Obama's first duty is to protect the citizens of the United States. Apart from protecting them from themselves, he has to protect them from outside attacks. This will be achieved by continuing the war against terrorists and controlling nuclear proliferation.

Because America is still the most powerful nation on earth, it is important for investors to pay close attention to their political aims and ambitions.

To make matters more complicated, elections in other countries do not coincide with those in the United States, so there is always something happening to concern investors. The UK is currently stable for another three years, albeit with a weak coalition government. Their main concern is tackling the deficit and the question of the future position of the UK within the European Union.

The European Union is still in an evolving stage. The biggest problem has been the divide between the members of the Euro

Currency Zone and the other ten members, like the UK, who are outside. They have also had to deal with the desperate situation in Greece, Spain, Portugal, and Ireland.

The main difference between the current US and European economic strategies is their completely opposite approach to lifting their economies out of recession.

The United States is sticking to the "Keynesian" theory of spending their way out, without worrying about increasing the debt, whereas Europe has instituted severe austerity measures to reduce debt. It is unlikely that both can be right, but only time will tell. It is a real economic enigma.

That is a very brief overview of the major democracies of the West. The Middle East is likely to remain in a state of total confusion for many years. The other important geographical area that concerns investors is Asia. The largest economic engine is now China, which is a republic but not like the Western republics. It is controlled by seven men who have truly autocratic powers. China will play a large part in the future as far as investment is concerned, but for now it is complicated by currency convertibility issues, lack of corporate governance, and limited visibility.

As far as economics is concerned, investors have to make their own assessments. We should only be guided by economists' forecasts, but I find it particularly difficult now because of the extreme difference that exists between America and Europe.

As I have previously stated, economics is an imprecise art, yet governments to some extent must be guided by the majority view. They juggle figures around to suit their purpose and can always blame unforeseen events if their policies to not work out.

One thing is certain: we will eventually rise out of the current recession and return to a period of inflation. Oh dear! The bane of all economists and politicians. Life is seldom smooth.

Do I have a theory to cope with these political and economic ups and downs? Well, yes I do. Apart from understanding the ups and downs due to political and economic conditions, it is necessary to determine what really destroys wealth and then devise a system that aims to minimise the effects.

There are two such destroyers. They are grey, like the warships of the same name. We will call them D1 and D2.

D1 is taxation. As the old saying goes "There are only two certainties in life: death and taxes". There is nothing we can do about the former, but we owe it to ourselves to minimise the latter. This book, as I have stated before, cannot advise on taxation because every nation, and every citizen within each nation, has different taxation issues to contend with.

The point to realise is that tax can play havoc with retirement plans. It is vital, therefore, to seek advice from a tax specialist, who can tell you the best way to minimise it by legal tax avoidance planning. I say "tax avoidance", which is very different from "tax evasion", which is illegal.

D2 is inflation. There are few periods where there is deflation, but even in severe recessions, such as the one we are in at the moment, inflation is running between 1½ and 2½ per cent. Our retirement planning must therefore take this into account.

So having decided how to best minimise taxation, we now need to plan our actual investments to cope with inflation. This is where the "Tilden theory" comes in. It is simply a strategy that aims to match, or beat, inflation on a total return basis. By total return, I mean a combination of income and capital appreciation.

Forget about beating all the other fund managers, beating indices, and beating forecasts. Simply concentrate on beating inflation. When you first start saving for your retirement, it will be a case of "What can I afford to put aside?" rather than "In order to build up a pot of £1 million, I need to save x amount per year". Whatever amount you do put aside, you will need to add an amount each year to match inflation.

It is unlikely that you will be in a position to invest a lot until your mortgage is paid off. On top of that, you may have substantial expenses for your children's education. Once these exceptional expenses are over, you will be in a better position to assess what your expenses will be when you retire.

You should sit down with your partner, if you have one, and write down a list of your fixed and variable expenses. Your pension planning should then commence in earnest. Do not overlook depreciation on motor vehicles, health insurance, and property maintenance.

On the other side of the equation is your pension (if you will receive one). There may be a state pension and possibly a corporate pension. The first question to ask yourself is, "Are they inflation linked?" If the answer is yes, then that is a great relief.

So the difference between your annual expenses and your guaranteed pensions is what you need to cover with your own investments.

During some years, you will be putting in more than you spend, using car depreciation as an example.

You will then have a net surplus, which you can either physically or figuratively put into a separate account. It will therefore be available when you require it without upsetting the original plan to maintain the level of total return needed to beat inflation.

The structure of an investment portfolio to achieve the desired result will vary with the economic cycle.

At this moment in time, with interest rates at their all time low in America and Europe, one area of investment that is unlikely to match inflation is the Treasury market or cash deposits. Yields are so low that they do not match inflation. As of November 2012, for instance, the yields on US and UK Treasuries were as follows:

	US	UK
5-year %	0.65	0.72
10-year %	1.61	1.73
20-year %	2.34	2.64
30-year %	2.75	3.08

These are redemption yields, which allow for capital losses if stock is over par (100) or gains if under par (100).

Inflation is currently fluctuating between 1½ and 2½ per cent, so only the longest dated bonds show a gross yield to redemption in excess of inflation.

Because inflation is not expected to rise until there is a strong economic recovery, interest rates are expected to remain low. However, when the recovery comes, there will inevitably be a rise in inflation.

Fortunately for my investment theory, rising inflation means rises in property assets and in stock prices. It is therefore essential to move out of fixed interest stocks and cash and into growth stocks and assets such as property. It may well be a year or more before the real recovery starts, so that is why my plan is to beat inflation over a seven-year period, which is roughly the average length of an economic interest rate cycle.

Normal investment should follow the same principles, but all too often investors, and particularly their advisers, are not nimble enough to miss the downturn or participate in the rise. Fund managers of specific funds really have their hands tied. For instance, a manager of an equity fund cannot go liquid to any great extent, or else there would be complaints. Most investors put money in an equity fund and expect the manager to be fully invested. If they want to hold 20 per cent of their assets in cash, they would only invest 80 per cent of their total funds in the equity fund. This is of course where the manager is caught between a rock and a hard place and why so many equity funds underperform.

I know that this is a flaw in the system. If I was going to market an equity fund, I would be sure to put in the fund prospectus that the manager may be up to 50 per cent liquid if market conditions warrant it. That way my fund would not be so volatile. Of course people may argue that I might miss some of the next rise in the market and therefore underperform. That is the difference between the fund manager who is worrying about underperformance compared to his peers, and me, whose sole concern is to beat inflation.

It is complete nonsense for a fund manager to crow about the fact his fund has beaten the benchmark index or some of his competitors' funds, if his fund has not matched or exceeded the rate of inflation.

Because equity markets tend to fall faster than rise, it is essential therefore to reduce exposure to volatile assets sooner rather than later. If an investor sells on the day the stock market peaks, or buys at its lowest point, it is sheer luck. The shrewd and experienced investor should, however, be able to recognise some of the signs that are always there, especially with hindsight. How can we change hindsight to foresight?

There are several good indicators. One that should be listened to carefully is the central bank's view of the economy and the likelihood of interest rates moving up or down. A company's interim and annual reports to shareholders can also give a clue as to the strength of corporate profits over the next reporting period. You have to understand that there is a big difference between a true cyclical stock, such as a commodity or manufacturing company, and a noncyclical stock, like a supermarket or utility company. The latter will not be as volatile; they are often called defensive stocks.

Another measure of the economic cycle, of course, is the unemployment rate, but this indicator is behind the event rather than ahead, like the first two. It does, however, confirm any doubts that one might have that a change is taking place.

Right now there are few signs that the world's economies are improving. European Union countries, as a bloc, have actually gone back into recession.

The American economy is likely to be the first to recover. In fact the first signs are already visible. The politicians have, to a large extent, buried their differences, and are conscious of the fact that the American people want them to work together on a solution to the economic problems. It will be difficult to maintain the recovery in isolation, so the rest of the world, especially Europe, will also need to recover. We are therefore likely to be about at the bottom of the economic cycle, and it is definitely time for me to continue acquiring equities with the cash that is earning pathetically low rates of interest. I have already locked in an average 5 per cent income from large cap equities in the UK. Not only has this income increased in the last two years, but the overall value of the portfolio is currently in profit. A lot of the investments are high yielding stocks such as utilities. My next purchases will be more cyclical and lower yielding but still above the rate of inflation. I know I may see the value of my portfolio go above or below cost, as we are still at the bottom of the cycle. I am, however, well positioned for a continuing level of income to match or beat current inflation and produce capital gains in due course. I appreciate that I may not reach my target of a total return in excess of inflation if the stock market falls this year, but my plan is to beat it over seven years.

I have managed to find some stocks currently yielding 3 per cent, which have excellent chances of rising as the economy recovers. I am not expecting to see a dramatic rise as the US Fed had indicated that it will not raise rates until 2015. It has also said it will not raise rates until unemployment falls to 6½ per cent or inflation goes above 2½ per cent. Nevertheless, as time passes and the economy recovers, there will be a sharp increase in equities as cash comes off the sidelines. Historically, the current depression is as bad as the 1930s, with unemployment rates in Spain, for instance, at 25 per cent.

There are differences, because socialism has introduced all sorts of benefits which did not exist then. As a result, there are no pictures of soup kitchens and barefoot children.

There are other types of investment which always get a boost when the stock markets are depressed. No doubt some of these are attractive. The obvious one is gold and other precious metals. Wine is another. They are not quite as attractive as their salespeople would have you believe, because there are storage and insurance costs and no interest or dividend. They are also in some instances not always easy to trade in. If you do feel you want to diversify your assets, it might be best to look at a collective investment vehicle, which would be easier than doing it yourself. I prefer stocks that pay dividends whilst waiting for possible capital appreciation, and usually they will beat other types of investment.

So, back to the "Tilden theory." You will by now know that it is related to inflation and only inflation, because not matching it will destroy your spending power.

Some individuals have, one way or another, accrued sufficient capital to produce the income required for retirement. Their only problem is to produce an after tax result to match or beat inflation. They are few and far between, and some of their wealth has probably come via an inheritance. Most individuals will be happy to be able to regularly set aside some money for their retirement.

The essential difference between them and the previous group is that if they are still working, they need to concentrate on building up their assets without any actual need for such assets to produce income. The thrust of their portfolio will be to achieve capital growth, so this means that there will be a bias towards cyclical rather than defensive stocks and only cash if the equity markets look too high and may well fall.

I have said that income is not important, but most companies pay dividends, so there will be a bonus to the capital growth plan.

I must mention that many companies offer investors a dividend reinvestment plan. You will receive some additional shares allocated to you; the number will be calculated by the net amount of the dividend being used to buy shares on the dividend payment date. If there is no deduction of standard rate tax on a dividend, the gross amount will be invested in new shares, but you will be liable for the tax.

It does offer a simple way of building up your stock holding, and there are no brokers' fees. People always complain about their cost of living rising without appreciating that it is the cost of inflation. In order to combat this, you should always buy shares in companies that cause your cost of living to rise. Buy an oil stock for the rise in your heating oil, buy a utility stock to cover your water and your electricity, and buy a supermarket stock to cover your food costs. The dividends you receive, plus capital growth, should go a long way to cover your additional costs!

There is no doubt that the earlier you start to save, the easier it will be to achieve your aims of a comfortable index-linked pension. To build it up, you should make regular monthly purchases of stocks or indices of your choice. That way, you will be dollar/pound cost averaging, which evens out the ups and downs. In 2012, for instance, if you were buying the index on the first of each month in the S&P 500 SPDR Units and the FTSE100 Index, you would have purchased as follows:

	SPDR	FTSE100		SPDR	FTSE100
January	1258.86	5572.30	July	1362.33	5571.10
February	1312.45	5681.60	August	1379.32	5635.30
March	1365.90	5871.50	September	1406.54	5711.50
April	1408.47	5768.50	October	1440.90	5742.10
May	1397.86	5737.80	November	1412.20	5782.70
June	1309.87	5320.90	December	1416.34	5866.80

Your average price for the S&P500 would have been 1372.59 and for the FTSE100 5688.51.

If you are busy, it may well be easier to buy an index fund or ETF, as there will be less accounting to do, and small amounts of individual stocks cost a lot more to buy. Once you have built up enough to invest £1,000 into, say, ten stocks, that would be more sensible. Even if you dealt through a dealing only company online, each £100 deal would cost you, say, £10 commission, where £1,000 would still cost you £10. Ten per cent or one per cent—quite a difference!

As I write, the creation of wealth is going to become harder for the following reasons. The whole world is going through a deep recession. All governments in Europe are instigating austerity measures, which are in danger of leading to anarchy in some countries, especially where unemployment is very high, like Spain. In order to try and balance budgets, the wealthy are an obvious source of additional revenue to governments; taxing them is politically popular but in fact, as they are such a low percentage of the population, the additional revenue is not great. The middle classes are where governments' main tax revenue comes from. In addition to income tax, there are many other sources of income such as VAT or sales tax and duties on fuel and cigarettes. The list goes on and on. This necessity for revenue is obviously due to government spending. Societies in the West have become used to free education, free healthcare, free this, that, and the other. In fact, as we all know, there is no such thing as a free lunch. Once we have these goodies, we are loathe to give them up or even see them cut back. Sadly, we are going to see some reductions in benefits; certainly, since we are living longer, the age when pensions will start will soon change.

In America, the current definition of a wealthy person is someone whose gross income is $400,000 per annum or more. That does sound a lot to 98 per cent of the population, who gross less! Most of the people earning that amount are professionals. They have had to study for many years to become qualified. They may also have had to pay back student loans. In their first ten years after graduating, most would have been earning a lot less than $250,000. They would also be living in more expensive houses and have two cars, so their outgoings would be high. Their net after tax and expenses (i.e., their savings) would not be very high, and they are the people we need.

The really wealthy, like sporting heroes and film stars, give us pleasure but are not needed in the same way. I think the definition of wealthy should be income in excess of $1,000,000. It is all very well for the Oracle of Omaha, Warren Buffett, to say he thinks the wealthy should be happy to pay a little more tax. He really is wealthy and would not notice the increase in tax, because he could not possibly spend all his income anyway. He is shrewd enough not to give his definition of wealthy, but I am sure it would most likely be someone earning over $1,000,000, not $250,000.

In the UK and Europe, there will be increases in many taxes other than income tax. Politicians are conscious of the fact that you and I concentrate our minds on our level of income tax and tend to forget all the other stealth taxes.

Whichever way they do it, an index is produced which incorporates all the cost of living expenses. There is the Retail Price Index (RPI) and the Consumer Price Index (CPI). The CPI is usually lower than the RPI because of its constituents, and it is the one being adopted by government agencies and corporations when deciding on their annual salary increases.

What I am really saying is that costs will only go one way and so therefore will inflation.

If, after all careful retirement planning, you still do not have enough saved, there is a way to increase disposable retirement income by reducing income tax. This would also avoid capital gains tax and inheritance tax, so beneficiaries will inherit considerably more.

To do this means making a dramatic change to your life; it most certainly will not suit the majority of higher rate taxpayers. The extremely wealthy, whose net income greatly exceeds their expenditure, would not be interested, and the poorer individuals living on state pensions and small income from savings could not afford to.

The people most likely to look seriously at such a plan would be the moderately wealth individuals who have sold (or are thinking of selling) their businesses. They may well have enough retirement income to cover their expenditure and so can live at a comfortable standard, yet they would be happier if they could increase it and preserve their assets for their children.

The dramatic change I refer to is, of course, to emigrate to a no tax or low tax jurisdiction. UK residents have been retiring abroad for years. Their favourite places tend to be the English-speaking islands of Guernsey, Jersey, and the Isle of Man. They are also very close to the

UK, whereas other favourite countries for tax and climatic reasons, like Spain, Portugal, and France, are further away. Nowadays, with the increase in air connections, the difference is not so great, but there are tax complications and language difficulties.

Although historically the British have been the keenest to emigrate for tax reasons and have had the benefit of being able to emigrate to the nearby islands, other nationals might also consider emigrating if taxation becomes too severe.

If we go back to the late 1960s, the British had a socialist government under the premiership of Harold Wilson. They introduced a punitive upper income tax rate of 98p in the pound. This led to the famous "brain drain", when many professionals such as doctors, surgeons, and businessmen, and music groups like the Beatles and the Rolling Stones left England for more favourable tax climes such as the USA and Australia. Britain at that time was extremely socialist, almost communist. Fortunately, common sense, a rare commodity, prevailed, and the rates of tax were lowered. This extreme case shows that there is a point of no return as far as taxing the wealthy is concerned.

Yet now, the French government, led by socialist President Hollande, have tried to introduce a 75 per cent tax rate on wealthy individuals. The US government under Democratic President Obama has just introduced a higher rate of tax on wealthy individuals and a higher rate of tax on dividends.

The definition of wealth varies, and it is quite interesting that in the case of the French, it is individuals with an income of €1.3M, whereas in America it is $400,000: a wide variation. Also the top tax rate in America is only 38.6 per cent, so it is not as penal as the French.

I do not propose delving deeply into tax issues, as this is outside the ambit of this book. I merely use it to show that there is a point at which some individuals will say enough is enough and vote with their feet. If you have decided you are at this point, you must really investigate all your options. The first is to make sure that you are paying as little tax as you have to by consulting a tax specialist. If the answer is that you are, then you and your spouse must agree that you both, in principle, want to emigrate.

You then need to seek specialist advice on each and every jurisdiction that you are considering moving to. The following points are important:

- rates of income tax
- capital gains tax
- wealth tax
- inheritance tax
- corporation tax
- property tax (rates)
- change of domicile (very specific advice needed)

There is no doubt that there are substantial financial advantages to moving out of the UK and France but less so in America. I do know that there are some Americans who make this move, but compared to the British, it is a very low percentage. Apart from financial reasons, some people retire to warmer climes. That is why Spain was so attractive to the British. The Americans, of course, do not need to emigrate for this reason; they can simply move to a southern state like Florida.

There are really three constituents to be juggled with to find the place that meets with most of the emigrants' wishes. They are financial, geographic, and climatic. There is no perfect place on earth, or we would all live there, and that would become a nightmare! The final selection will be a place with the biggest number of ticks on your list of priorities.

I must emphasise that emigration is an extreme solution and one which most people will turn down outright, because they want to be close to their family and friends. They also have established social and sporting activities which may have to be given up if they move.

Because it is such an emotive decision, I cannot emphasise enough that it is so important to make plans early in your adult life to provide you with enough capital and income to retire comfortably without considering emigrating.

The "Tilden theory" of personal pension planning is capable of achieving the results you need. The earlier you start saving, the better; you should make serious retirement investment plans in your late twenties or when you get married, whichever comes first. I hope this little book will guide you to success, and that you will keep referring to it as your life progresses.

Now the investment lesson is over, the activation of your pension plan is in your capable hands. The sun is setting behind the palm trees, and it is time for my evening gin and tonic. So I will say, "Good health and farewell"!

Visit the author's website www.affluentman.co.uk for information regarding regular updates on politics, economics and investment strategy.

About the Author

Tim Tilden-Smith is a Fellow of the Chartered Institute for Securities and Investment. He is a director of an investment company and a property company; and chairman of Services International Limited. He founded a document storage business, which is a division of Services International Limited, and trades under the name of Archivist. All these companies are registered in Guernsey, Channel Islands.

He lives in Guernsey but spends the winter months in Florida, with his American wife. His hobbies are messing about in boats, golf, and gardening.

Lightning Source UK Ltd.
Milton Keynes UK
UKOW05f0244070913

216725UK00001B/40/P